Mometrix TEST PREPARATION

I0893677

Texas Massage Therapy Written Exam Secrets Study Guide

DEAR FUTURE EXAM SUCCESS STORY

First of all, **THANK YOU** for purchasing Mometrix study materials!

Second, congratulations! You are one of the few determined test-takers who are committed to doing whatever it takes to excel on your exam. **You have come to the right place.** We developed these study materials with one goal in mind: to deliver you the information you need in a format that's concise and easy to use.

In addition to optimizing your guide for the content of the test, we've outlined our recommended steps for breaking down the preparation process into small, attainable goals so you can make sure you stay on track.

We've also analyzed the entire test-taking process, identifying the most common pitfalls and showing how you can overcome them and be ready for any curveball the test throws you.

Standardized testing is one of the biggest obstacles on your road to success, which only increases the importance of doing well in the high-pressure, high-stakes environment of test day. Your results on this test could have a significant impact on your future, and this guide provides the information and practical advice to help you achieve your full potential on test day.

Your success is our success

We would love to hear from you! If you would like to share the story of your exam success or if you have any questions or comments in regard to our products, please contact us at **800-673-8175** or **support@mometrix.com**.

Thanks again for your business and we wish you continued success!

Sincerely,
The Mometrix Test Preparation Team

Need more help? Check out our flashcards at:
http://MometrixFlashcards.com/NCBTMB

Written and edited by the Mometrix Exam Secrets Test Prep Team
Printed in the United States of America

Table of Contents

Introduction

Thank you for purchasing this resource! You have made the choice to prepare yourself for a test that could have a huge impact on your future, and this guide is designed to help you be fully ready for test day. Obviously, it's important to have a solid understanding of the test material, but you also need to be prepared for the unique environment and stressors of the test, so that you can perform to the best of your abilities.

For this purpose, the first section that appears in this guide is the **Secret Keys**. We've devoted countless hours to meticulously researching what works and what doesn't, and we've boiled down our findings to the five most impactful steps you can take to improve your performance on the test. We start at the beginning with study planning and move through the preparation process, all the way to the testing strategies that will help you get the most out of what you know when you're finally sitting in front of the test.

We recommend that you start preparing for your test as far in advance as possible. However, if you've bought this guide as a last-minute study resource and only have a few days before your test, we recommend that you skip over the first two Secret Keys since they address a long-term study plan.

If you struggle with **test anxiety**, we strongly encourage you to check out our recommendations for how you can overcome it. Test anxiety is a formidable foe, but it can be beaten, and we want to make sure you have the tools you need to defeat it.

Secret Key #1 – Plan Big, Study Small

There's a lot riding on your performance. If you want to ace this test, you're going to need to keep your skills sharp and the material fresh in your mind. You need a plan that lets you review everything you need to know while still fitting in your schedule. We'll break this strategy down into three categories.

Information Organization

Start with the information you already have: the official test outline. From this, you can make a complete list of all the concepts you need to cover before the test. Organize these concepts into groups that can be studied together, and create a list of any related vocabulary you need to learn so you can brush up on any difficult terms. You'll want to keep this vocabulary list handy once you actually start studying since you may need to add to it along the way.

Time Management

Once you have your set of study concepts, decide how to spread them out over the time you have left before the test. Break your study plan into small, clear goals so you have a manageable task for each day and know exactly what you're doing. Then just focus on one small step at a time. When you manage your time this way, you don't need to spend hours at a time studying. Studying a small block of content for a short period each day helps you retain information better and avoid stressing over how much you have left to do. You can relax knowing that you have a plan to cover everything in time. In order for this strategy to be effective though, you have to start studying early and stick to your schedule. Avoid the exhaustion and futility that comes from last-minute cramming!

Study Environment

The environment you study in has a big impact on your learning. Studying in a coffee shop, while probably more enjoyable, is not likely to be as fruitful as studying in a quiet room. It's important to keep distractions to a minimum. You're only planning to study for a short block of time, so make the most of it. Don't pause to check your phone or get up to find a snack. It's also important to **avoid multitasking**. Research has consistently shown that multitasking will make your studying dramatically less effective. Your study area should also be comfortable and well-lit so you don't have the distraction of straining your eyes or sitting on an uncomfortable chair.

The time of day you study is also important. You want to be rested and alert. Don't wait until just before bedtime. Study when you'll be most likely to comprehend and remember. Even better, if you know what time of day your test will be, set that time aside for study. That way your brain will be used to working on that subject at that specific time and you'll have a better chance of recalling information.

Finally, it can be helpful to team up with others who are studying for the same test. Your actual studying should be done in as isolated an environment as possible, but the work of organizing the information and setting up the study plan can be divided up. In between study sessions, you can discuss with your teammates the concepts that you're all studying and quiz each other on the details. Just be sure that your teammates are as serious about the test as you are. If you find that your study time is being replaced with social time, you might need to find a new team.

Secret Key #2 – Make Your Studying Count

You're devoting a lot of time and effort to preparing for this test, so you want to be absolutely certain it will pay off. This means doing more than just reading the content and hoping you can remember it on test day. It's important to make every minute of study count. There are two main areas you can focus on to make your studying count.

Retention

It doesn't matter how much time you study if you can't remember the material. You need to make sure you are retaining the concepts. To check your retention of the information you're learning, try recalling it at later times with minimal prompting. Try carrying around flashcards and glance at one or two from time to time or ask a friend who's also studying for the test to quiz you.

To enhance your retention, look for ways to put the information into practice so that you can apply it rather than simply recalling it. If you're using the information in practical ways, it will be much easier to remember. Similarly, it helps to solidify a concept in your mind if you're not only reading it to yourself but also explaining it to someone else. Ask a friend to let you teach them about a concept you're a little shaky on (or speak aloud to an imaginary audience if necessary). As you try to summarize, define, give examples, and answer your friend's questions, you'll understand the concepts better and they will stay with you longer. Finally, step back for a big picture view and ask yourself how each piece of information fits with the whole subject. When you link the different concepts together and see them working together as a whole, it's easier to remember the individual components.

Finally, practice showing your work on any multi-step problems, even if you're just studying. Writing out each step you take to solve a problem will help solidify the process in your mind, and you'll be more likely to remember it during the test.

Modality

Modality simply refers to the means or method by which you study. Choosing a study modality that fits your own individual learning style is crucial. No two people learn best in exactly the same way, so it's important to know your strengths and use them to your advantage.

For example, if you learn best by visualization, focus on visualizing a concept in your mind and draw an image or a diagram. Try color-coding your notes, illustrating them, or creating symbols that will trigger your mind to recall a learned concept. If you learn best by hearing or discussing information, find a study partner who learns the same way or read aloud to yourself. Think about how to put the information in your own words. Imagine that you are giving a lecture on the topic and record yourself so you can listen to it later.

For any learning style, flashcards can be helpful. Organize the information so you can take advantage of spare moments to review. Underline key words or phrases. Use different colors for different categories. Mnemonic devices (such as creating a short list in which every item starts with the same letter) can also help with retention. Find what works best for you and use it to store the information in your mind most effectively and easily.

Secret Key #3 – Practice the Right Way

Your success on test day depends not only on how many hours you put into preparing, but also on whether you prepared the right way. It's good to check along the way to see if your studying is paying off. One of the most effective ways to do this is by taking practice tests to evaluate your progress. Practice tests are useful because they show exactly where you need to improve. Every time you take a practice test, pay special attention to these three groups of questions:

- The questions you got wrong
- The questions you had to guess on, even if you guessed right
- The questions you found difficult or slow to work through

This will show you exactly what your weak areas are, and where you need to devote more study time. Ask yourself why each of these questions gave you trouble. Was it because you didn't understand the material? Was it because you didn't remember the vocabulary? Do you need more repetitions on this type of question to build speed and confidence? Dig into those questions and figure out how you can strengthen your weak areas as you go back to review the material.

Additionally, many practice tests have a section explaining the answer choices. It can be tempting to read the explanation and think that you now have a good understanding of the concept. However, an explanation likely only covers part of the question's broader context. Even if the explanation makes perfect sense, **go back and investigate** every concept related to the question until you're positive you have a thorough understanding.

As you go along, keep in mind that the practice test is just that: practice. Memorizing these questions and answers will not be very helpful on the actual test because it is unlikely to have any of the same exact questions. If you only know the right answers to the sample questions, you won't be prepared for the real thing. **Study the concepts** until you understand them fully, and then you'll be able to answer any question that shows up on the test.

It's important to wait on the practice tests until you're ready. If you take a test on your first day of study, you may be overwhelmed by the amount of material covered and how much you need to learn. Work up to it gradually.

On test day, you'll need to be prepared for answering questions, managing your time, and using the test-taking strategies you've learned. It's a lot to balance, like a mental marathon that will have a big impact on your future. Like training for a marathon, you'll need to start slowly and work your way up. When test day arrives, you'll be ready.

Start with the strategies you've read in the first two Secret Keys—plan your course and study in the way that works best for you. If you have time, consider using multiple study resources to get different approaches to the same concepts. It can be helpful to see difficult concepts from more than one angle. Then find a good source for practice tests. Many times, the test website will suggest potential study resources or provide sample tests.

Practice Test Strategy

If you're able to find at least three practice tests, we recommend this strategy:

Untimed and Open-Book Practice

Take the first test with no time constraints and with your notes and study guide handy. Take your time and focus on applying the strategies you've learned.

Timed and Open-Book Practice

Take the second practice test open-book as well, but set a timer and practice pacing yourself to finish in time.

Timed and Closed-Book Practice

Take any other practice tests as if it were test day. Set a timer and put away your study materials. Sit at a table or desk in a quiet room, imagine yourself at the testing center, and answer questions as quickly and accurately as possible.

Keep repeating timed and closed-book tests on a regular basis until you run out of practice tests or it's time for the actual test. Your mind will be ready for the schedule and stress of test day, and you'll be able to focus on recalling the material you've learned.

Secret Key #4 – Pace Yourself

Once you're fully prepared for the material on the test, your biggest challenge on test day will be managing your time. Just knowing that the clock is ticking can make you panic even if you have plenty of time left. Work on pacing yourself so you can build confidence against the time constraints of the exam. Pacing is a difficult skill to master, especially in a high-pressure environment, so **practice is vital**.

Set time expectations for your pace based on how much time is available. For example, if a section has 60 questions and the time limit is 30 minutes, you know you have to average 30 seconds or less per question in order to answer them all. Although 30 seconds is the hard limit, set 25 seconds per question as your goal, so you reserve extra time to spend on harder questions. When you budget extra time for the harder questions, you no longer have any reason to stress when those questions take longer to answer.

Don't let this time expectation distract you from working through the test at a calm, steady pace, but keep it in mind so you don't spend too much time on any one question. Recognize that taking extra time on one question you don't understand may keep you from answering two that you do understand later in the test. If your time limit for a question is up and you're still not sure of the answer, mark it and move on, and come back to it later if the time and the test format allow. If the testing format doesn't allow you to return to earlier questions, just make an educated guess; then put it out of your mind and move on.

On the easier questions, be careful not to rush. It may seem wise to hurry through them so you have more time for the challenging ones, but it's not worth missing one if you know the concept and just didn't take the time to read the question fully. Work efficiently but make sure you understand the question and have looked at all of the answer choices, since more than one may seem right at first.

Even if you're paying attention to the time, you may find yourself a little behind at some point. You should speed up to get back on track, but do so wisely. Don't panic; just take a few seconds less on each question until you're caught up. Don't guess without thinking, but do look through the answer choices and eliminate any you know are wrong. If you can get down to two choices, it is often worthwhile to guess from those. Once you've chosen an answer, move on and don't dwell on any that you skipped or had to hurry through. If a question was taking too long, chances are it was one of the harder ones, so you weren't likely to get it right anyway.

On the other hand, if you find yourself getting ahead of schedule, it may be beneficial to slow down a little. The more quickly you work, the more likely you are to make a careless mistake that will affect your score. You've budgeted time for each question, so don't be afraid to spend that time. Practice an efficient but careful pace to get the most out of the time you have.

Secret Key #5 – Have a Plan for Guessing

When you're taking the test, you may find yourself stuck on a question. Some of the answer choices seem better than others, but you don't see the one answer choice that is obviously correct. What do you do?

The scenario described above is very common, yet most test takers have not effectively prepared for it. Developing and practicing a plan for guessing may be one of the single most effective uses of your time as you get ready for the exam.

In developing your plan for guessing, there are three questions to address:

- When should you start the guessing process?
- How should you narrow down the choices?
- Which answer should you choose?

When to Start the Guessing Process

Unless your plan for guessing is to select C every time (which, despite its merits, is not what we recommend), you need to leave yourself enough time to apply your answer elimination strategies. Since you have a limited amount of time for each question, that means that if you're going to give yourself the best shot at guessing correctly, you have to decide quickly whether or not you will guess.

Of course, the best-case scenario is that you don't have to guess at all, so first, see if you can answer the question based on your knowledge of the subject and basic reasoning skills. Focus on the key words in the question and try to jog your memory of related topics. Give yourself a chance to bring the knowledge to mind, but once you realize that you don't have (or you can't access) the knowledge you need to answer the question, it's time to start the guessing process.

It's almost always better to start the guessing process too early than too late. It only takes a few seconds to remember something and answer the question from knowledge. Carefully eliminating wrong answer choices takes longer. Plus, going through the process of eliminating answer choices can actually help jog your memory.

Summary: Start the guessing process as soon as you decide that you can't answer the question based on your knowledge.

How to Narrow Down the Choices

The next chapter in this book (**Test-Taking Strategies**) includes a wide range of strategies for how to approach questions and how to look for answer choices to eliminate. You will definitely want to read those carefully, practice them, and figure out which ones work best for you. Here though, we're going to address a mindset rather than a particular strategy.

Your odds of guessing an answer correctly depend on how many options you are choosing from.

Number of options left	5	4	3	2	1
Odds of guessing correctly	20%	25%	33%	50%	100%

You can see from this chart just how valuable it is to be able to eliminate incorrect answers and make an educated guess, but there are two things that many test takers do that cause them to miss out on the benefits of guessing:

- Accidentally eliminating the correct answer
- Selecting an answer based on an impression

We'll look at the first one here, and the second one in the next section.

To avoid accidentally eliminating the correct answer, we recommend a thought exercise called **the $5 challenge**. In this challenge, you only eliminate an answer choice from contention if you are willing to bet $5 on it being wrong. Why $5? Five dollars is a small but not insignificant amount of money. It's an amount you could afford to lose but wouldn't want to throw away. And while losing $5 once might not hurt too much, doing it twenty times will set you back $100. In the same way, each small decision you make—eliminating a choice here, guessing on a question there—won't by itself impact your score very much, but when you put them all together, they can make a big difference. By holding each answer choice elimination decision to a higher standard, you can reduce the risk of accidentally eliminating the correct answer.

The $5 challenge can also be applied in a positive sense: If you are willing to bet $5 that an answer choice *is* correct, go ahead and mark it as correct.

Summary: Only eliminate an answer choice if you are willing to bet $5 that it is wrong.

Which Answer to Choose

You're taking the test. You've run into a hard question and decided you'll have to guess. You've eliminated all the answer choices you're willing to bet $5 on. Now you have to pick an answer. Why do we even need to talk about this? Why can't you just pick whichever one you feel like when the time comes?

The answer to these questions is that if you don't come into the test with a plan, you'll rely on your impression to select an answer choice, and if you do that, you risk falling into a trap. The test writers know that everyone who takes their test will be guessing on some of the questions, so they intentionally write wrong answer choices to seem plausible. You still have to pick an answer though, and if the wrong answer choices are designed to look right, how can you ever be sure that you're not falling for their trap? The best solution we've found to this dilemma is to take the decision out of your hands entirely. Here is the process we recommend:

Once you've eliminated any choices that you are confident (willing to bet $5) are wrong, select the first remaining choice as your answer.

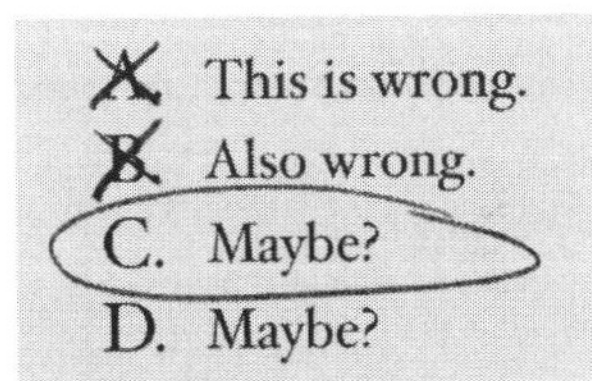

Whether you choose to select the first remaining choice, the second, or the last, the important thing is that you use some preselected standard. Using this approach guarantees that you will not be enticed into selecting an answer choice that looks right, because you are not basing your decision on how the answer choices look.

This is not meant to make you question your knowledge. Instead, it is to help you recognize the difference between your knowledge and your impressions. There's a huge difference between thinking an answer is right because of what you know, and thinking an answer is right because it looks or sounds like it should be right.

Summary: To ensure that your selection is appropriately random, make a predetermined selection from among all answer choices you have not eliminated.

Test-Taking Strategies

This section contains a list of test-taking strategies that you may find helpful as you work through the test. By taking what you know and applying logical thought, you can maximize your chances of answering any question correctly!

It is very important to realize that every question is different and every person is different: no single strategy will work on every question, and no single strategy will work for every person. That's why we've included all of them here, so you can try them out and determine which ones work best for different types of questions and which ones work best for you.

Question Strategies

✓ Read Carefully

Read the question and the answer choices carefully. Don't miss the question because you misread the terms. You have plenty of time to read each question thoroughly and make sure you understand what is being asked. Yet a happy medium must be attained, so don't waste too much time. You must read carefully and efficiently.

✓ Contextual Clues

Look for contextual clues. If the question includes a word you are not familiar with, look at the immediate context for some indication of what the word might mean. Contextual clues can often give you all the information you need to decipher the meaning of an unfamiliar word. Even if you can't determine the meaning, you may be able to narrow down the possibilities enough to make a solid guess at the answer to the question.

✓ Prefixes

If you're having trouble with a word in the question or answer choices, try dissecting it. Take advantage of every clue that the word might include. Prefixes can be a huge help. Usually, they allow you to determine a basic meaning. *Pre-* means before, *post-* means after, *pro-* is positive, *de-* is negative. From prefixes, you can get an idea of the general meaning of the word and try to put it into context.

✓ Hedge Words

Watch out for critical hedge words, such as *likely, may, can, often, almost, mostly, usually, generally, rarely*, and *sometimes*. Question writers insert these hedge phrases to cover every possibility. Often an answer choice will be wrong simply because it leaves no room for exception. Be on guard for answer choices that have definitive words such as *exactly* and *always*.

✓ Switchback Words

Stay alert for *switchbacks*. These are the words and phrases frequently used to alert you to shifts in thought. The most common switchback words are *but, although*, and *however*. Others include *nevertheless, on the other hand, even though, while, in spite of, despite*, and *regardless of*. Switchback words are important to catch because they can change the direction of the question or an answer choice.

⊘ Face Value

When in doubt, use common sense. Accept the situation in the problem at face value. Don't read too much into it. These problems will not require you to make wild assumptions. If you have to go beyond creativity and warp time or space in order to have an answer choice fit the question, then you should move on and consider the other answer choices. These are normal problems rooted in reality. The applicable relationship or explanation may not be readily apparent, but it is there for you to figure out. Use your common sense to interpret anything that isn't clear.

Answer Choice Strategies

⊘ Answer Selection

The most thorough way to pick an answer choice is to identify and eliminate wrong answers until only one is left, then confirm it is the correct answer. Sometimes an answer choice may immediately seem right, but be careful. The test writers will usually put more than one reasonable answer choice on each question, so take a second to read all of them and make sure that the other choices are not equally obvious. As long as you have time left, it is better to read every answer choice than to pick the first one that looks right without checking the others.

⊘ Answer Choice Families

An answer choice family consists of two (in rare cases, three) answer choices that are very similar in construction and cannot all be true at the same time. If you see two answer choices that are direct opposites or parallels, one of them is usually the correct answer. For instance, if one answer choice says that quantity x increases and another either says that quantity x decreases (opposite) or says that quantity y increases (parallel), then those answer choices would fall into the same family. An answer choice that doesn't match the construction of the answer choice family is more likely to be incorrect. Most questions will not have answer choice families, but when they do appear, you should be prepared to recognize them.

⊘ Eliminate Answers

Eliminate answer choices as soon as you realize they are wrong, but make sure you consider all possibilities. If you are eliminating answer choices and realize that the last one you are left with is also wrong, don't panic. Start over and consider each choice again. There may be something you missed the first time that you will realize on the second pass.

⊘ Avoid Fact Traps

Don't be distracted by an answer choice that is factually true but doesn't answer the question. You are looking for the choice that answers the question. Stay focused on what the question is asking for so you don't accidentally pick an answer that is true but incorrect. Always go back to the question and make sure the answer choice you've selected actually answers the question and is not merely a true statement.

⊘ Extreme Statements

In general, you should avoid answers that put forth extreme actions as standard practice or proclaim controversial ideas as established fact. An answer choice that states the "process should be used in certain situations, if..." is much more likely to be correct than one that states the "process should be discontinued completely." The first is a calm rational statement and doesn't even make a definitive, uncompromising stance, using a hedge word *if* to provide wiggle room, whereas the second choice is far more extreme.

⊘ BENCHMARK

As you read through the answer choices and you come across one that seems to answer the question well, mentally select that answer choice. This is not your final answer, but it's the one that will help you evaluate the other answer choices. The one that you selected is your benchmark or standard for judging each of the other answer choices. Every other answer choice must be compared to your benchmark. That choice is correct until proven otherwise by another answer choice beating it. If you find a better answer, then that one becomes your new benchmark. Once you've decided that no other choice answers the question as well as your benchmark, you have your final answer.

⊘ PREDICT THE ANSWER

Before you even start looking at the answer choices, it is often best to try to predict the answer. When you come up with the answer on your own, it is easier to avoid distractions and traps because you will know exactly what to look for. The right answer choice is unlikely to be word-for-word what you came up with, but it should be a close match. Even if you are confident that you have the right answer, you should still take the time to read each option before moving on.

General Strategies

⊘ TOUGH QUESTIONS

If you are stumped on a problem or it appears too hard or too difficult, don't waste time. Move on! Remember though, if you can quickly check for obviously incorrect answer choices, your chances of guessing correctly are greatly improved. Before you completely give up, at least try to knock out a couple of possible answers. Eliminate what you can and then guess at the remaining answer choices before moving on.

⊘ CHECK YOUR WORK

Since you will probably not know every term listed and the answer to every question, it is important that you get credit for the ones that you do know. Don't miss any questions through careless mistakes. If at all possible, try to take a second to look back over your answer selection and make sure you've selected the correct answer choice and haven't made a costly careless mistake (such as marking an answer choice that you didn't mean to mark). This quick double check should more than pay for itself in caught mistakes for the time it costs.

⊘ PACE YOURSELF

It's easy to be overwhelmed when you're looking at a page full of questions; your mind is confused and full of random thoughts, and the clock is ticking down faster than you would like. Calm down and maintain the pace that you have set for yourself. Especially as you get down to the last few minutes of the test, don't let the small numbers on the clock make you panic. As long as you are on track by monitoring your pace, you are guaranteed to have time for each question.

⊘ DON'T RUSH

It is very easy to make errors when you are in a hurry. Maintaining a fast pace in answering questions is pointless if it makes you miss questions that you would have gotten right otherwise. Test writers like to include distracting information and wrong answers that seem right. Taking a little extra time to avoid careless mistakes can make all the difference in your test score. Find a pace that allows you to be confident in the answers that you select.

✓ KEEP MOVING

Panicking will not help you pass the test, so do your best to stay calm and keep moving. Taking deep breaths and going through the answer elimination steps you practiced can help to break through a stress barrier and keep your pace.

Final Notes

The combination of a solid foundation of content knowledge and the confidence that comes from practicing your plan for applying that knowledge is the key to maximizing your performance on test day. As your foundation of content knowledge is built up and strengthened, you'll find that the strategies included in this chapter become more and more effective in helping you quickly sift through the distractions and traps of the test to isolate the correct answer.

Now that you're preparing to move forward into the test content chapters of this book, be sure to keep your goal in mind. As you read, think about how you will be able to apply this information on the test. If you've already seen sample questions for the test and you have an idea of the question format and style, try to come up with questions of your own that you can answer based on what you're reading. This will give you valuable practice applying your knowledge in the same ways you can expect to on test day.

Good luck and good studying!

Anatomy and Physiology

Anatomy

Anatomy is the study of the structures that make up a body, organism, or any living thing. Anatomy is derived from the Greek term "anatomia", meaning to cut up or cut open. With reference to the human body, it can be divided into the study of different sections such as torso or head, or of the various systems of the body such as the circulatory or respiratory systems. Physiology is the study of the various functions of the body to include the mechanical, biochemical, and physical functions of the body. Histology refers to the study of microscopic tissue that has been thinly sliced, possibly stained, and then mounted on a slide for further study. Kinesiology is the science of the movement of the body. This study takes into account a background in biology, human anatomy, physiology, biomechanics, and overall human health. Pathology is the study of the processes leading to diseases such as cancer, or other health abnormalities.

Human organisms

At the basic level, all massage therapists must have an elementary understanding of the anatomy and physiology of the human body. The smallest particles that make up the body consist of atoms or ions. These are comprised of carbon, hydrogen, oxygen, and nitrogen. At the next level, atoms make up molecules within the body. Arranged in a specific manner, molecules form into compounds and matter known as cells. Cells are the basic units that make up all living things. Cells are organized into tissues that can consist of epithelial, nervous, muscle, or connective tissue. Tissues comprise organs in the body such as the lungs, heart, kidneys, and liver. These organs are further grouped into systems, for example, the circulatory system, the respiratory system, and the digestive system. Finally, all of the listed components make up an organism. The study of the structure of an organism or body is known as morphology.

Cells

Cells are the basic units that make up all living things. Human beings, plants, animals, and even bacteria consist of specialized cells that perform highly regulated functions. Cells consist of protoplasm, which is the gelatinous matter within a cell that houses important elements such as protein, fats, carbohydrates, mineral salts, and water. Cells differ in their shape and size as they are specialized to perform a specific function within the body. Cells are composed of cytoplasm, nucleus, and a cell membrane. The passage of wastes and nutrients are made through this membrane that also serves as a doorway into the cell. Within the center of the cell lies the nucleus, surrounded by the cytoplasm. The nucleus is highly dense while the cytoplasm is less so. The cytoplasm contains distinct areas called the cytoplasmic organelles that perform the following functions: determining the supply of food, water, and oxygen and also eliminating waste and other toxins. The cytoplasm also is responsible for maintaining the proper temperature level for optimal survival. Without these in place, the cell cannot grow and will most certainly die.

Activities

The purpose of cells is determined during differentiation. Each cell is designed to perform one of three activities: vegetative, growth and reproduction, or specialized. The vegetative process involves the cell's removal of waste products as well as the absorption of nutrients and other maintenance activities. Cellular activities relating to growth and reproduction consist of cellular mitosis. This activity also encompasses cellular differentiation. As a result of differentiation, cells are assigned specialized functions within the organism. This cellular activity is further broken down into the type of function each cell is expected to perform. For example, cells composing muscular tissue must have the ability to contract or lengthen. Cells associated with nerve endings must continually reproduce to replace those that may become damaged. Also, skin cells replace ones that die off and are sloughed off the body from daily activities.

DIFFERENTIATION AND CELLULAR MITOSIS

From its beginnings as a fertilized egg, a single cell begins the process of division into specialized cells that have specific, unique functions. These cells as a group are undergoing a process known as differentiation, whereby they develop into their final purpose within the organism. When the body has fully developed tissues and organs, the cells do not live forever, but are continually being replaced through a process known as cellular mitosis. In this division, cells are replicated into daughter cells, or like cells, that have the same distinct characteristics and function as the parent cells. In one example, cells that continually are replaced, such as skin cells, are indistinguishable from one another. To reach complete cellular mitosis, five steps must occur before the process results in a second similar cell. These steps are known as interphase, prophase, metaphase, anaphase, and telephase.

During interphase, the cell readies itself for division. While continually growing, the cell produces proteins and cytoplasmic organelles. During prophase, the DNA within the cell becomes larger and more defined. The cell's nuclear membrane disappears during this stage. During metaphase, the chromosomes become aligned in what is known as an equatorial plane, an imaginary line equidistant from the centrosome poles. During anaphase, the cell splits the chromatids back into chromosomes and they migrate towards opposite ends of the cell. Finally, during telophase, the cell completes the process of division, creating a new nuclear membrane to house the chromosomes, resulting in an exact duplicate of the parent cell containing the same genetic material.

METABOLISM, ANABOLISM, AND CATABOLISM

Metabolism is the cellular processes by which the cells intake nutrients, expel wastes, and perform their intended activities or functions. Essentially all chemical processes performed by the cell are metabolic. The breakdown of proteins, carbohydrates, or fats is part of the metabolic process. Anabolism is one of the phases of metabolism. In an anabolic state, energy is used by the cells to build up amino acids and other substances into more complex organic compounds such as enzymes. During the next stage, catabolism, the larger molecules are broken down into smaller components to produce energy. One byproduct of this process is to regenerate ATP: adenosine triphosphate, which stores energy until it is ready to be released.

TISSUES

Tissues, which are composed of groups of cells that carry out similar functions, are found in every organ within the body. Tissues can be categorized into five main groups depending on their function.

- Epithelial – This type of tissue serves a protective function and can be further divided based on the shape or number of layers of cells.
- Connective – This type of tissue is the framework for binding together structures.
- Muscular – This type of tissue is responsible for pulling together, or contracting, elongated cells, thereby causing body parts to move.
- Nervous – This type of tissue is composed of nerve cells which are primarily located within the brain, spinal cord, and other nerves, acting as a channel by which messages are sent to and from the brain.
- Liquid – This type of tissue is best represented by blood and lymph that ends up circulating throughout the body removing wastes and absorbing nutrients.

Epithelial Tissue

The primary purpose of epithelial tissue is to form a protective layer or barrier against infections. This tissue also assists in the process of absorption, excretion of wastes, secretion of fluids, and also protection from bacteria or injury. This type of tissue is found covering all surfaces of the body, over the organs, and within the interior lining of the same organs. Depending on the location, this tissue can be further classified into the following groups. Squamous cells are flat cells, generally one cell thickness. Cuboidal cells are square shaped and can be many layers thick. Columnar cells are tall and rectangular. Stratified squamous cells are several layers thick and transitional squamous cells are generally flatter and closely packed together.

Connective Tissue

Connective tissue allows parts to be bound together within the body. These tissues also help to provide the structural framework of the body. Connective tissue, called areolar tissue, serves to connect the skin to other tissues and helps to fill the spaces within muscles. This tissue is found beneath the dermis and is also present within the digestive track and under all epithelial tissue. This tissue is also referred to as superficial fascia. It contains numerous blood cells and nerves. Another type of connective tissue is adipose tissue that is composed primarily of fat cells called adipocytes. Its function is to protect against heat loss and to store energy for the body. Primarily found in the largest quantities in the abdominal region, it can also exist near the heart muscle, around the kidneys, and most anywhere underneath the skin. Excess adipose tissue around the centralized region of a person's body is an indicator of potential health risks to include cardiovascular disease and diabetes mellitus.

Fascia

Fascia is the connective tissue that surrounds all portions of the body from the skin, muscles, bones and joints. It serves a protective purpose while also lubricating and providing shape and support to the body. This fascia is built of a fibrous network made of elastin and collagen within a gel substance. It helps the body to move while reducing the possibility of irritation. The fascia layer just beneath the skin is known as the superficial fascia. Deep fascia is located around each muscle tissue and fiber. This allows the muscles to move independently while also contracting together as a unit. This deep fascia also helps to attach muscles to bone. Subserous fascia is located between deep fascia and the membranes that line the internal cavities of the body. This helps to fill in some of the gaps while still allowing for slight movement of the internal organs.

Muscle Tissue

The main purpose of muscle tissue is to contract the fibers that compose the muscles allowing that body part to move. The first type of muscle tissue is skeletal muscle. Tendons attach these muscles to the bones and help to control movement through conscious effort by the person using impulses sent from the brain, through the nerves, and finally into the muscle. Due to this method of transmission, these skeletal muscles are referred to as voluntary muscles. The cells of these muscles are long and similar to threads with dark and light markings on them known as striations. Such muscles are known as striated muscles. A second type of muscle tissue is called smooth muscle. Generally this type is non-striated and cannot be induced to contract through voluntary means. One example of this can be found in the way that food is transmitted through the digestive tract. A third type of muscle tissue is cardiac muscle tissue, found only in the heart. It functions involuntarily and helps to pump blood throughout the body by way of arteries and veins through cardiac contractions.

Tissue Repair

Surface tissue and skin generally exhibit the least amount of recuperative time to heal and return to their original state. Deeper tissues such as those within muscles take longer to heal and require more in depth stretching, friction, and massage techniques performed in those areas. Bones and ligaments tend to heal slowly while muscles and tendons heal with considerable scarring and some loss of elasticity and strength. Portions of the central nervous system that have been injured or traumatized often do not heal at all. Correct techniques for the type of injury have been shown to alleviate pain as well as strengthen the muscles, ligaments, and tendons, thereby decreasing the amount of scar tissue formed. Development of scar tissue results from connective tissue cells that have entered the area of injury developing a fiber network by which regenerative tissue bonds create scar tissue. It is important to minimize the amount of scar tissue in one area in order to prevent excessive buildup that can inhibit movement and range of motion.

Membranes

Membranes serve the purpose of being the outermost layer of a cell providing the barrier between the interior of the cell to the outside. Membranes are divided into two main categories: epithelial membranes and fibrous connective tissue membranes. Epithelial membranes have an outer covering of epithelium, while fibrous connective tissue membranes are composed of binding fibers and a thick gel substance. There are two types of epithelial membranes: mucous and serous membranes. Mucous membranes manufacture a thick substance that helps protect and lubricate the cells and tissues. Serous membranes produce a liquid that also serves to lubricate. The main serous membranes present in the body are the pleura, pericardium, and the peritoneum. Other membranes within the body are the skeletal membrane, the perichondrium and the synovial membrane.

Anatomical Positions

There are three main planes: sagittal, coronal, and transverse; also referred to by: superior or inferior, anterior or posterior, and medial, lateral, distal, and proximal. When the body is face forward with palms facing up, an imaginary line is drawn vertically down the body dividing it into left and right halves. This is referred to as sagittal. When the body is divided into front and back halves, it is referred to as coronal. Finally, when the body is divided into upper and lower halves, it is referred to as transverse. Cranial is a synonym for superior, while caudal can be interchanged with inferior. Anterior is also a synonym for ventral, and posterior can be interchanged with dorsal. Medial refers to any portion that pertains to the midline of the body. Lateral refers to the part of the body furthest from the midline, or center. Distal is referenced when speaking of the parts of the body furthest from a point of attachment. Proximal refers to the parts of the body nearest to the point of attachment.

Anterior Regions

The anterior regions of the human body are:

- Frontal – head
- Temporal – temples
- Cervical – neck
- Deltoid – shoulder area
- Axillary - armpit
- Brachial – area between elbow and shoulder
- Hypochondrium – abdominal area lateral from epigastric region
- Umbilical – area between the navel and pubic region

- Hypogastric – area under the stomach and above the umbilical region
- Patellar – knees and kneecap
- Femoral – femur or thigh
- Inguinal – groin
- Epigastric – abdominal region
- Pectoral – chest area

Posterior Regions

The posterior regions of the human body are:

- Occipital – back of the head
- Parietal – the head, posterior to the frontal, yet anterior to the occipital
- Mastoid – behind the ear
- Cervical – neck
- Scapular – back of the shoulder or shoulder blade
- Lumbar – lower back
- Sacral – below the lumbar region and between the gluteal
- Gluteal – buttock muscles
- Popliteal – area behind the knee

Anatomical Parts

The human body is divided into distinct regions: head, spine, trunk, and extremities. The region of the head encompasses the skull, face, eyes, nose, mouth, and chin. The spinal region is made up of the bones that support the head and trunk of the body such as the vertebrae. The region of the trunk is divided into additional subcategories. These include the thoracic region, or chest encompassing the rib cage, heart, lungs, esophagus, and parts of the trachea. The second subsection is comprised of the abdominal area containing the stomach, kidneys, liver, intestines, and the diaphragm. The final region of the body is the extremities. These are the upper limbs: the shoulders, arms, wrists, and hands, as well as the lower limbs: the hips, thighs, legs, knees, ankles, and feet.

Body Cavities and Organs

The ease of which one can recall the location of body organs is based upon prior knowledge of the body's planes. The main body cavities are as follows: cranial, spinal, thoracic, abdominal, and pelvic. The cranial cavity encompasses anything relating to the skull. The spinal cavity deals with the portion of the body relating to the spinal column and the vertebrae. The thoracic cavity is divided into two sections, each focusing on the heart and lungs, respectively. The abdominal cavity, the portion of the body located below the diaphragm, encompasses the liver, stomach, pancreas, spleen, and the intestines. Finally, the pelvic cavity houses parts of the reproductive system, bladder, and rectum. Dorsal cavities are the cranial and spinal cavities. Ventral cavities are the thoracic, abdominal, and pelvic.

Organ Systems

Organ systems within the body are defined as those organs that work together to perform a specific function. The list is as follows:

- Integumentary System
- Skeletal System
- Muscular System

- Circulatory System
- Nervous System
- Endocrine System
- Digestive System
- Respiratory System
- Excretory System
- Reproductive System

Functions

- Integumentary system (the skin): largest organ in the body; responsible for *protecting* the internal structure of the body, *regulating* the body's temperature, absorption and excretion, and sensation of touch. Organs: the epidermis, dermis, and the sebaceous glands.
- The skeletal system: 206 bones; responsible for providing the framework of the body; connected to one another and to the muscles through ligaments and tendons.
- The muscular system: voluntary and involuntary muscles; provide capacity for movement, digestion of food, and contractions of the heart muscle.
- The circulatory system: vessels carry blood throughout the body; originate from the heart muscle, through the arteries, veins, capillaries, lymph nodes and lymph vessels; ensures that oxygen and nutrients are delivered to cells.
- The nervous system: the brain, spinal cord, and nerves that emanate from these areas throughout the body.
- The endocrine system is composed of organs or glands that regulate the release of hormones that can affect the overall health of the individual. The glands that relate to this system are the thyroid, pituitary, pancreas, ovaries and testes.
- The digestive system is made up of the mouth, esophagus, stomach, liver, intestines, and the gallbladder. These organs aid in processing food into a substance that is able to be utilized by the cells in the body.
- The respiratory system is made up of the nasal passages, pharynx, trachea, bronchi, and lungs. Their role is to assist the body with absorbing oxygen into the bloodstream and aid it in the release of carbon dioxide.
- The excretory system consists of the kidneys, bladder, urethra, liver, large intestines and the entire urinary tract system. The sole purpose is to eliminate wastes from the body.
- The reproductive system is responsible for ensuring that the human organism has the ability to reproduce with the aid of the ovaries, uterus, fallopian tubes, vagina, penis, seminal vesicles, and testes.

Skin

The primary functions of the skin are:

- Protective barrier from the outside and to prevent any harmful bacteria, fungus, or other elements from invading the body; protects the internal organs from damage or injury.
- Regulate the body's temperature by maintaining the internal temperature at around 98.6 degrees Fahrenheit. (Releases excess heat via sweat glands; makes adjustments in the skin to keep the body warm).
- Secrete fluids, oils, water, and perspiration. (Helps regulate temperature, moisturize the skin, keeps excess water from entering the pores.)
- Allows sensation of touch and other sensations such as heat, cold, pressure, and pain.

- Allows for absorption (ex: nutrients from lotions, creams, and topical medications.
- Respiration through the skin (pores have a minimal ability to allow oxygen in and to release carbon dioxide).

STRUCTURE OF THE SKIN

A cross section of the skin shows the various layers which comprise the protective sheath over all human organisms. The skin is made of the epidermis and the dermis. The epidermis is the outermost layer and the dermis makes up the deeper layer called the subcutaneous tissue. The epidermis is composed of a layer of skin cells in varying degrees of thickness depending on which part of the body it covers. For example, the soles of the feet have thicker skin than the area covering the earlobes. The epidermis is made up of several layers of cells: stratum corneum, stratum lucidum, stratum granulosum, stratus spinosum, and the stratum germinativum. The dermis is composed of a mixture of cells as well as water, fibers and a gel-like substance called "ground." There are several types of fibers present in the dermis: collagen, reticulum, and elastin. Collagen gives the skin its shape, form, strength, and flexibility, while reticulum provides the fibrous structure to the skin and the elastic provides resiliency. The dermis itself contains the papillary layer, made up of capillaries and tactile corpuscles, and the reticular layer, made up of fat cells, hair follicles, nerve endings, and sweat glands.

NUTRITION AND AGING

In order for the skin to be properly hydrated and able to perform the function of protecting the body, it is important that nutrients continue to be absorbed through the skin. These nutrients are responsible for assisting in the repair of damaged skin cells, hair and nails. Within the body, up to about half the total volume of blood and lymph can be found in the skin. Capillaries, arteries, hair papillae, and glands make their home in the subcutaneous layer of the skin. During the process of aging, the skin gradually loses its elasticity and tends to droop or sag. It is less firm and more likely to undergo visual changes such as an increase in lines, spots, or growth. The skin may swell in areas under the eyes leading to puffiness. Sagging occurs as the skin loses its resiliency and buoyancy and leads to droopiness under the arms and along the jaw line.

PRIMARY AND SECONDARY LESIONS

Lesions are defined as any structural change in the surface of the skin that may be caused by an injury or a potential disease. Medical terminologies of certain types of primary lesions are: bulla, macule, tubercule, papule, pustule, ulcer, tumor, vesicle, and wheal.

Secondary lesions: scar, crust, scale, fissure, excoriation

POTENTIAL STRUCTURAL CHANGES

While performing a massage, it is important to differentiate between healthy skin and skin which has surface damage or internal damage to the underlying tissue. Birth marks such as port-wine stains, strawberry marks, freckles, and moles generally present no challenges to the therapist. However, occasionally a patient's skin may be sensitive to the touch, temperature or exhibit other signs of injury not visible to the naked eye. Any lesions or open sores should be pointed out to the patient prior to the commencement of the massage and also a referral to a physician may be warranted if the therapist feels that it deserves medical attention. At no time should the massage therapist make a hypothesis as to a medical diagnosis for the patient. These injured areas in particular should be avoided during the massage. Skin that is healthy should feel moist, soft, and supple to the touch and appear smooth when undergoing a visual check. Skin pigment due to production of melanin is not an indicator of damaged skin; however, the skin should have an overall good color and not look ashy, pale, reddish, or have a yellow cast to it.

Skin Blemishes or Injuries

- Acne and blackheads: Acne can appear most often on the face, back, or chest of a person and usually is the result of overactive sebaceous glands. They can also be the direct result of hormonal changes such as those encountered during pregnancy. Blackheads are the result of clogged sebaceous glands and are also partnered with pimples.
- Bruises (or contusions): result of injured skin where blood vessels have broken and blood has pooled underneath the skin, but has not broken through. This is usually due to strike or blow to the skin.
- Impetigo: common childhood condition in which a bacterial skin infection develops primarily around the mouth. This takes on the appearance of crusty pustules and is highly contagious.
- Rosacea: expresses itself through excessive oiliness and also through redness around the cheek and nose area sometimes covered with small pustules. The pores become enlarged and also the skin becomes coarse.
- Warts (common, venereal, or plantar): Common warts are traditionally found on the hands while plantar warts tend to grow inward on the soles of the feet causing great pain.

Decubitus Ulcers

A decubitus ulcer is more commonly known as a bedsore or pressure sore. It can be the result of a person being confined to a bed for long periods of time, or a person who may be confined to a wheelchair without adequately shifting positions. A pressure sore tends to form over an area where there is a bony projection and not enough underlying tissue to cushion the area. Lack of blood supply, oxygen, and nutrients to the area coupled with the lack of circulation causes a red spot to form and then eventually become ulcerated. This open wound may then become infected. With the assistance of a massage therapist, the areas near the sore can be massaged; however, the exact location should be avoided. Massage will assist with maintaining circulation within the area and potentially help prevent pressure sores from developing.

Skin Cancers or Tumors

With the prevalence of individuals who have used tanning beds as well as the greater number of outdoor activities experienced today, it is important for the therapist to become familiar with the types of skin cancers that are commonly found. Of utmost importance is that the massage therapist does not attempt to replace a client's primary care physician in trying to diagnose these skin diseases. There are three types of skin cancers. The first is basal cell carcinoma. This cancer appears as a small raised bump or nodule that sometimes is pus-filled. It is slow to develop and is most prevalent in lighter skinned individuals. A second type of skin cancer is squamous cell carcinoma. This type is made up of red papules. This type has the ability to metastasize and gain a stronghold in deeper tissues. It can also form a raised nodule that exhibits scaling and crust then repeats the process. Both of these types of cancers are treated through freezing methods. A third type of skin cancer is a malignant melanoma. A dark patch of skin that generally appears near an existing mole and changes its shape indicates this cancer. It is a highly aggressive form of skin cancer and has the highest fatality rate of the three. A tumor is defined as an abnormal tissue growth in the skin. The location of a tumor can vary from the surface of the body to anywhere within an internal organ. Most tumors are benign, however, they warrant a check by a physician just to be sure.

Venereal Diseases and Herpes

Certain venereal diseases are communicable through sexual contact and it's important for the massage therapist to practice methods to ensure his own safety when working with a client who has one of these diseases. These diseases affect the sexual organs and can produce rashes, lesions, or sores on the outside of the skin as well as internal. Syphilis produces sores on the body that have an open crater in the center. It is highly contagious and even when it appears to have gone away, can also produce a secondary rash capable of spreading to other areas of the body. Gonorrhea is another disease affecting the sexual organs. This disease causes painful urination, burning sensations, and a discharge but otherwise can show no other symptoms. Untreated, this disease can cause the transmission of harmful bacteria into the bloodstream. Herpes is also another highly contagious infection that is viral in nature. While there is no cure, outbreaks can be controlled with medication as can abstention from sexual relations. Herpes can exist in two forms: type I or type II. Type I is exhibited as the more common cold sore. Type II is also known as genital herpes. Another form of herpes is known as herpes zoster, or shingles. This type is an infection caused by the chicken pox virus and produces painful areas on the body and also pus-filled blisters.

ALLERGIC REACTIONS

Allergies are defined as a skin disorder characterized by increased sensitivity to a type of topical cream, lotion, or cosmetic, or by sensitivities to certain foods or insects. Allergies are identified as generally a skin rash, edema, redness, blisters, or itchy scaly skin. Common skin allergies include:

- Eczema – Inflammation of the skin often accompanied by redness, scales, and blisters. Can be either in acute or chronic form.
- Dermatitis – Also an inflammatory condition that sometimes produces lesions that may be filled with pus.
- Contact dermatitis – Generally presents itself when a person comes into contact with a substance such as a certain metal, chemicals such as food dyes or hair dyes, or household cleaners.
- Psoriasis – A condition that also produces dry scaly patches of the skin, often on the legs, arms, chest, and back. This condition is not contagious, but massage in that area should be avoided due to possibility of bleeding to occur.
- Urticaria – More commonly known as hives. This condition can occur as a result of an allergic reaction or through emotional stress. Severe itches, raised legions or welts are an indicator of presence of hives. Though not contagious, massage in this region should be avoided.

SKIN PIGMENTATIONS

The color of one's skin is determined by the amount of melanin that is present in the dermis as well as outside forces such as the amount of time that is spent in the sun, on a tanning bed, or on the types of medications taken internally. For the massage therapist, generally darker skinned individuals do not exhibit as much sensitivity to a massage as a lighter skinned person due to the increased potential for sunburns on fairer skin. Types of pigmentation structures to look for include lentigines, or freckles, stains, such as brown patches, chloasma, such as liver spots, commonly found on the face, neck, or cheeks. Also, naevus, which are also called birthmarks, leucoderma, or abnormal light skin patches, or albinism, which is the absence of melanin in the skin, are all types of skin pigmentations. Lack of melanin in albino individuals affects the color of the hair, eyes, and skin and makes the person susceptible to sunburns.

Skeletal System

The skeletal system consists of calcified structures under the skin that combine to form the framework for the human body. The skeletal system serves five main functions. They are:

1. Provide the framework and offer support to our bodies. The skeleton also gives our body its shape.
2. To serve as an additional form of protection to the internal organs which are situated within the interior of this structure.
3. To provide a place for muscles to attach and to aid with movements of the body's limbs and appendages.
4. To assist in the production of red blood cells which are formed in bone marrow.
5. To serve as a storage facility for minerals such as calcium phosphate, sodium, and magnesium.

Review Video: Skeletal System
Visit mometrix.com/academy and enter code: 256447

Types of Bones

There are four types of bone identified as part of the skeletal system: long bones, which are those found in the arms, legs, and fingers, and short bones, such as those found in the carpals of the hand and tarsals of the foot. Pelvic bones, skull bones and ribs make up the flat bones. Finally, irregular bones make up the fourth type. These bones are called vertebrae and are located in the spinal area. Although the bone is considered a hard substance within the body, it is constantly evolving through regeneration. Bone is made up of about 33% animal, or organic matter, and 67% mineral or earthy matter. Organic matter consists of bone cells, blood vessels, connective tissue and bone marrow. Minerals found within the bones are calcium phosphate and calcium carbonate.

Long Bone Characteristics

A long bone is made up of a multitude of layers with each end being larger than the middle section allowing this bone to move in conjunction with the bone nearest to it. The end of the bone is referred to as the epiphysis and is covered with a layer of cartilage called the articular cartilage, the purpose being to provide an area of shock absorption. The long portion of the bone between the epiphysis is known as the diaphysis. The overall covering of the bone that is visible is called the periosteum, a network of fibers that protects the bone and is the area that tendons and ligaments attach. The next layer is made up of compact bone tissue, which actually forms the hard portion of the bone. The inner layer is called spongy bone. Bone marrow is located within this area and it is the region where red blood cells are produced. Spongy bone is named for the reason that it consists of empty spaces separated by thin bony plates. The medullary cavity, a hollow chamber, contains the yellow bone marrow.

Axial vs. Appendicular Skeleton

The axial skeleton is comprised of the head and trunk areas of the human body. It is further broken down into the following regions: cranium, face, hyoid bone, ear, vertebral column, and the thoracic cage. The purpose of the axial skeleton is to protect the areas of vital organs located within the body. There are approximately 80 separate bones contained within this skeletal system. The appendicular skeleton controls the movements of the upper and lower extremities. It is composed of the following structures: shoulder girdle, arm, hand, pelvic girdle, leg, and foot. There are a total of 126 separate bones located within this system. Although these bones move more freely than the axial skeleton, it is important for the massage therapist to consider any limitations in range of motion when performing a massage. The human body consists of 206 bones as a result of these two skeletal systems.

CONNECTIONS

The bones cannot move independently and require assistance from muscles, tendons, and ligaments to work together and cause the bones of the body to move in a single direction. The areas where the muscles and tendons attach are known as the joints. Joints are divided into several categories depending on the amount of motion that they allow. Synarthrotic joints are found in the skull and have no mobility. Amphiarthrotic have limited movement and can be found at the base of the spine and the top of the pelvic area. They are also found in the pubic region. Diarthrotic joints are able to move freely. Examples would be the ball and socket joints found in the scapula/humerus area, hinge joints and gliding joints commonly found near the knee. Bones that meet at the ends of these joints are covered with articular cartilage. A capsule like shape envelops the joint, providing a membrane in which synovial fluid is produced to lubricate the joint area and allow more fluid motions to occur.

BONE FRACTURES

A fracture is defined as a separation of the bone into two or more parts, generally caused through injury or stress of the bone beyond its capabilities. There are four main types of fractures, dependent upon the degree of breakage. The first type, most commonly seen in younger children, is known as a greenstick fracture. This type of fracture does not break through the bone completely, but causes a fracture line part way through. It receives its name similar to the breaking of a young tree branch. The bone is still soft and contains much cartilage, which contributes to the incomplete fracture. A second type of fracture is called a closed or simple fracture. In this type, the fractured bone does not pierce the skin. The break generally occurs along a single line and splits the bone neatly in two. An open or compound fracture involves the puncture of the bone through the surface of this skin. This type requires a thorough cleanup of the puncture site to prevent contamination of the bone from bacteria. Compound fractures generally require surgery and antibiotic treatment. A fourth type of fracture is comminuted. This type results in the breaking of the bone into many small pieces and also requires surgery to attach pins to strengthen the bones as they heal.

CARTILAGE, LIGAMENTS, AND BURSAE

Cartilage is an elastic substance composed of connective tissue whose main purpose is to provide a cushion for joints. Cartilage is located in a gel-like substance called the matrix. This matrix does not contain any blood vessels and therefore nutrients are diffused through the matrix into the cartilage. Cartilage can be found in the earlobe, the area between the ribs, the nose, and the bronchial tubes. Ligaments are fibrous tissues that connect bones together. Not to be confused with tendons that connect muscles to bones, ligaments connect to form a joint. They are composed of fibrous connective tissue and allow or disallow for certain range of motions. When ligaments are stretched beyond their limitations, a dislocation can occur. It is important to reset a dislocated appendage as soon as possible so the ligament does not remain stretched out causing increased instability. Bursae are the fluid filled sacs located near a joint that assists in reducing the amount of friction present in the joint. They are present throughout the body anywhere joints are located and prevent bones from rubbing together. Inflammation of the bursa is referred to as bursitis.

HERNIATED DISK

A herniated disk is an invertebral disk that has protruded out into the spinal cavity causing increased pressure and pain on the spinal cord. This disk could also cause radiating pressure and pain on the nerve endings leading down the legs. Most commonly occurring in the lumbar region, the typical herniated disk occurs gradually over time. When seeing a physician for this condition, diagnostic tests may be ordered to determine the degree of severity. These tests can include x-ray, myelogram, CT scan, and MRI to determine the exact cause of the pain as the symptoms produced can mimic other illnesses or diseases. Initial treatment of a herniated disk includes hot or cold therapy, massage, exercises, stretches, rest, pain medication, and in severe or prolonged cases, surgery.

Strain vs. Sprain

A strain is an injury that occurs when a muscle has been stretched beyond its capabilities. It can also be referred to as a pulled muscle. Microscopic tears within the muscle cause pain, stiffness, swelling, and sometimes bruising. A sprain is an injury that occurs when a ligament is overstretched suddenly causing pain, immediate swelling and bruising. Severe sprains involve a popping, either felt or heard, and loss of function of that body part. There are three main classifications of sprains. The first is identified as a class I sprain, where the ligament has stretched out, but there is relatively no loss of the limb's function. The second is a class II sprain in which the ligament is torn and there is some degree of function loss with this injury. Some internal bleeding may occur, or there may not be any bruising or discoloration indicated. The third type, class III sprain, involves a complete tear of the ligament along with internal bleeding and extensive loss of function of the affected limb. All three types of sprains best heal using the R.I.C.E. method: rest, ice, compression, and elevation. Massage is recommended only for the latent stages of healing to help prevent the formation of scars and to increase range of motion and flexibility.

Arthritis

Arthritis is a condition resulting in inflammation of the joints. It leads to eventual structural changes to the bone. Arthritis can be detected through simple blood tests that look for the presence of arthridities. Slower movements, stiffness, swelling in the joints and less use of affected limbs are indicators of the presence of arthritis. The most prevalent form of arthritis is osteoarthritis. It is degenerative in nature and often is one sign of aging. Knees, hips, and the spine are areas that are most commonly affected. There is no cure, but treatments exist to ease the severity of symptoms and keep the joints flexible. A second type of arthritis is rheumatoid arthritis. This disease is a chronic autoimmune disease producing crippling, hot joints. There is no cure for this disease that results in calcification of the joints leading to eventual immobility.

Osteoporosis

Osteoporosis is a disease in which the bone mineral density is reduced and a higher incidence of fractures occurs. This disease affects more women than men, oftentimes affecting those with smaller frames. The bones produce and store calcium up until the mid 30's at which point, the body starts to slowly break down the minerals within the bones, causing greater propensity towards fractures. A person's lifestyle can also affect the likelihood of developing osteoporosis due to habits such as smoking, poor diet, lack of exercise, and alcohol abuse. There is some degree of genetic disposition towards this disease. Without any known symptoms of osteoporosis, the first indicator may be a fracture, at which time a bone density test may be performed to indicate the levels of calcium and minerals in the bones. A diet rich in calcium and vitamin D along with a non-sedentary lifestyle can also help prevent or postpone this disease.

Review Video: Osteoporosis
Visit mometrix.com/academy and enter code: 421205

Curvature of the Spine

A healthy spine should be in the form of a double S curve. The cervical and lumbar areas of the spine are concave and the thoracic area should be convex. Deviations from this S curve cause problems that can affect the overall health of the individual. A severely deformed spinal column can cause pressure on the nerve endings of the body, inhibit movement and produce a decrease in flexibility. Lack of strength and ability to absorb shocks can affect the day-to-day life for a person. If the spine is left untreated, permanent damage can occur as the body adjusts to the abnormal strain placed upon it. One type of curvature is known as scoliosis in which the spine shifts position laterally and causes the body to lean to the side. The shoulders and hips fall out of alignment. A second time is lordosis in which the spine is curved in an exaggerated concave shape. A third type is kyphosis. Occurring in the thoracic region, this type of curvature results in a "humped-back" shape. These abnormalities can be the result of poor posture, inherited defects, or be a sign of aging.

Muscular System

Muscles are considered organs within the muscular system. They are composed of cells and fibers that have the ability to stretch, lengthen, and constrict depending on the needs of the human body. Muscles are responsible for the movement of the human body in coordination with the brain through the sending of signals to the body. Muscles are the basis for all movement such as walking, flexing arms, grasping, breathing, and digesting food. They also are responsible for the beating of the heart and the passage of the blood through the body. Muscles help to provide shape to the skeletal system and keep the body in an upright position. When taken into account all the muscles within the body, they make up approximately 40% to 60% of a person's total body weight. Within the body, there are over 600 different muscles each with their own specific functions. Muscles utilize energy from the food we eat and the oxygen we breathe. By using this energy, the muscle is able to provide movement and helps to keep our bodies warm. When muscles get overexerted and pushed beyond limitations, it is important to consider massage as this act benefits muscles in the release of toxins from the body.

Review Video: Muscular System
Visit mometrix.com/academy and enter code: 967216

Muscular Tissue

The three types of muscular tissue are called skeletal, smooth, and cardiac. Skeletal muscle is also called striated muscle due to the presence of the tiny grooves of muscle located along one single major muscle group. Skeletal muscles are also voluntary muscles in that it takes a conscious effort to make the muscle perform the action requested. This is performed through the involvement of the central nervous system and the nerves that flow from the brain to each area of the body. Smooth muscles are involuntary muscles. They are made up of cells that are nonstriated and form fibrous bands. These muscles are commonly found lining the stomach, intestines, and also within blood vessels. They are involuntary and their movement is controlled by the autonomic nervous system. This type of muscle is not attached to any portion of the skeletal system. It works more slowly than other muscle tissue and does not readily fatigue. The third type of cardiac muscle is found within the heart. This muscle is also striated and under microscopic views, shows that the cells are quadrangular in shape and are joined together and supported through connective tissue.

Muscle Movements

Muscles are able to perform the functions of their job due to certain characteristics. These are known as irritability, contractility, elasticity and extensibility. Irritability refers to the ability of the muscles to be able to receive and react to stimuli from outside the body, such as the touch of massage, or internally, through electrical currents sent from the brain. The muscle's irritability also refers to the reaction from heat, chemicals such as acids or salts, or other impulses. Contractility refers to muscles which are capable of shortening and thus, exerting force. An example of contractility is the actions taken by the cardiac muscle which forces blood to the body due to the pumping action of the heart. Elasticity of a muscle refers to its ability to return to the original shape after being stretched. Extensibility is the ability of the muscle to stretch beyond its original shape.

Muscle Support

Skeletal muscles are those which are striated and are attached to the bones through tendons. When muscles constrict or expand, they cause a reaction on the tendon to either pull or push the bone causing movement of the limb or appendage. Tendons are not as elastic as the muscles, so the majority of the movement is achieved by the muscle. Skeletal muscles are primarily voluntary, however, they do have some involuntary characteristics that can also make the muscle contract or expand. Massage focuses on a therapeutic regimen designed to enhance the function of muscles through techniques that bring about relaxation, release of toxins, greater flexibility, range of motion, etc. All of which is accomplished through specific pressurized movements on the body.

Skeletal Muscle Tissue

Skeletal muscle tissue is composed of fibrous tissue arranged in bundles called fascicles. These fascicles are made up of muscle fibers connected to one another through connective tissue. An extensive supply of blood and lymph vessels, capillaries, and nerve fibers are contained within. The muscle receives its supply of oxygen through the blood vessels. There are two types of skeletal muscle fibers: type I and type II. Type I muscle fibers are characterized by a large number of reddish fibers which are excellent for providing endurance to the muscle through the presence of oxidative metabolism. Type II fibers appear white and are more suitable for shorter burst of energy or speed. They utilize anaerobic metabolism and are more ready to tire. The type of muscular fiber one has is determined through genetics and through training.

Point of Insertion

Muscles are connected by way of tendons extending from either end of the muscle. In order to provide for movement, one side of the muscle, generally the part closest to the center of the body, is considered the point of origin. This area is not as flexible as the other end of the muscle due to the lack of space in the area, and also a broader range of motion is not necessary from that area. At the other end of the muscle lies the insertion point. This area is more distal and the majority of the movement takes place here. Both the origin and the insertion point of the muscle attach to the bone by way of a tendon. When one knows the origin of the muscle, it is easy to infer which way the muscle will contract based on that knowledge.

Isometric and an Isotonic Contraction

When reviewing the ways that muscles contract and expand, it is important to note the differences between the types of contractions a muscle can perform. An isometric contraction occurs when the muscle is contracting; however, no increase in the length of the muscle can be seen. The muscle being isolated is tensed and the corresponding body part does not move. An isotonic contraction occurs when the muscle contracts and the distance from one end of the muscle to the other end has changed. The majority of the voluntary movements the body makes are considered isotonic. Isometric contractions are responsible for keeping the body in an upright position. An example of an isometric contraction would be when a person puts considerable strength against a heavy object, yet it still does not move. This tension one feels within the body is considered an isometric contraction. When a person is doing regular physical exercise such as running, the muscles are in an isotonic contraction.

PRIME MOVER

Although muscles are distinct within the body, they work in conjunction with other muscles to perform an action. As such, the muscle performing the primary movement is known as the prime mover, or the agonist. To counteract this initial movement, a muscle on the opposite side causes an opposite reaction. This muscle is known as the antagonist. As an example of this process, a bicep contraction is the agonist, while the expansion of the triceps would be considered the antagonist. It is important to understand the relationship between the muscles in this manner so as to create an appropriate treatment plan that takes the movement of both muscles under consideration. Any muscles that are involved with assisting the prime mover are called synergists. A fixator is any muscle which helps to stabilize a body part so another muscle has the ability to move.

MUSCLE SPASM

A muscle spasm is a dysfunction of the muscle in which involuntary contractions occur to a single muscle or to a group of muscles. The degree of intensity can vary based on the person's pain tolerance and how long the contractions continue. These spasms are classified as either tonic when they continue in the contraction state for some time, or clonic, when the spasm relaxes between contractions. Another term for muscle spasm is cramp. Typical kinds of spasms include hiccups, charley horses, twitches, and convulsions. Muscles can also spasm as a result of nearby injuries. In treating a spasm, it is not recommended to massage the direct area until the acute spasm has subsided. It is thought that compression on the ends of the muscle or prevention of the contraction of the antagonist muscles will help quiet the muscle under spasm. Massage after the acute phase has passed will help to eliminate toxins from the muscle and introduce nutrients to the area and restore circulation.

MUSCLE STRAINS

Muscle strains can also be referred to as torn or pulled muscles. There are generally three degrees of strains that can occur to the muscle. A grade 1 strain is where the muscle fibers have been overextended with very little tears in the fibers. This is pain, however, no visual marks on the surface of the skin. There is also no loss of function. A grade 2 strain shows partial tears occurring in less than 50% of the muscle fibers. There is pain, tenderness, inflammation, and some degree of loss of function. A grade 3 strain consists of more than 50% of the muscle fibers being torn. There is considerable pain and the bleeding may be seen under the skin. Swelling and immediate loss of muscle function occurs. To rehabilitate from these kinds of injuries involves use of the R.I.C.E. method (rest, ice, compression, and elevation) and massage once the acute stage has passed. It is important to maintain range of motion and flexibility once this stage is over to prevent muscle atrophy and reduce scarring.

HYPERTROPHY AND ATROPHY

As a muscle increases in size, it invariably gets larger. As seen in bodybuilders, the size of the muscle increases through repeated strength training. This effect of an increase in the width of a muscle is known as hypertrophy. The muscular fibers themselves do not increase in number, however, the size of the fibers increase in width. This increase leads to greater strength of the body part affected by the muscle, causing it to have more power while performing the required action or movement. Other increases that can be seen are an increase in the level of blood supply to the hypertrophic muscle and also an increase in ATP and mitochondria. Atrophy of a muscle refers to the disuse of a muscle causing it to degenerate and waste away. Muscles that are not used break down and shrink, gradually losing their strength. The amount of blood being supplied to the limb decreases, causing a change in the color of the limb. Atrophy commonly occurs in individuals with paralysis who have lost nerve connections to the muscles causing them to waste away.

Diseases That Affect the Muscular System

- Tendonitis: tendon that connects the muscle to the bone becomes inflamed.
- Tenosynovitis: inflammation that occurs along the tendon sheath. Symptoms: pain, stiffness, and swelling of the affected area. Treatment: massage, ice to decrease swelling, and physical manipulation to increase range of motion and assist with prevention of scar tissue.
- Lupus: autoimmune disease that can affect tissues and organs. This disease affects the connective tissue and can cause pain throughout many areas of the body. With this disease, blood vessels may become inflamed and arthritis can occur. Massage therapy on a person with lupus should be performed under the supervision of a physician to prevent pain to the patient.
- Fibromyalgia: affects the connective tissue, producing pain, stiffness, and fatigue in the muscles, tendons, and ligaments. Outside factors such as temperature, humidity, and infections can cause an increase in the person's discomfort level and trigger additional symptoms. With the pain levels of each person varying, it is important to coordinate a massage plan with the client's personal physician.
- Muscular dystrophy: causes progressive degeneration of the muscles in the body.

Blood

The average male human body is made up of about 11 pints of blood. Blood is a fluid filled with nutrients which travels through all areas of the body supplying these nutrients to muscles, bones, ligaments, skin cells, etc. The blood is responsible for bringing oxygen, water, and food to the body. The blood is also able to remove carbon dioxide and waste products from the body and send them through the excretory system to be eliminated from the body. The blood also helps to regulate the temperature of the body to maintain an average of 98.6 degrees Fahrenheit. When the body is injured, white blood cells within the vessels travel to the injured region to aid with healing. The red blood cells provide needed iron and help with coagulation for areas that are losing blood through hemorrhage. Blood is a type of connective tissue made up of 50-60% plasma.

Movement of the Scapula

The scapula is located on the posterior upper region of the body serving to connect the arm bone to the collarbone. The scapula is also known as the shoulder blade while the collarbone is referred to as the clavicle. The trapezius muscle is connected to the cervical spine from the occipital bone at the top of the spine down to the T5-T12 area of the lumbar column. Three types of trapezius muscles exist: upper, middle, and lower. Each corresponds to the region in which the muscles originate. These muscles are involved with the elevation or depression and upward rotation of the scapula. The rhomboid major originates from the T2-T5 portion of the thoracic vertebral column. It is located deep within the trapezius muscle. The purpose of the rhomboid major is to keep the scapula in line with the ribcage. The action instigated by this muscle is to pull the scapula closer to the vertebral column. The rhomboid minor also acts to retract the scapula downward. Its origin is between the C7-T1 vertebral column and the insertion is at the base of the scapula.

Terms

Levator Scapulae, pectoralis minor, and serratus anterior are three muscles that act upon the scapula in addition to the trapezius and rhomboid.

- Levator scapulae – This muscle originates from the C1-4 vertebral column, located at the back and side of the neck. It helps to move the neck from side to side laterally. It inserts at the top third of the scapula.

- Pectoralis minor – This muscle originates between the 3rd and 5th ribs close to the costal cartilage. The action of the pectoralis minor is to draw the scapula downward and towards the thorax. It attaches on the coracoid process that extends outward from the scapula.
- Serratus anterior - This muscle originates from the anterior ribs 1-8 and causes an upward movement of the scapula. It provides stabilization and is also referred to as the "boxer's muscle" because it assists with protraction of the scapula.

Pectoralis Major

The pectoralis major is divided into two groups, the clavicular portion and the sternal portion. The clavicular portion originates medially at the clavicle and inserts at the outer ridge of the bicipital groove. The action it causes is to conduct adduction, or movement of the limb closer towards the body, medial rotation, and flexion of the humerus bone. The humerus is the long bone extending from the scapula at the shoulder to the radius and ulna at the elbow. The sternal portion of the pectoralis major originates from the sternum and the costal cartilage of ribs 1-6 but inserts at the outer ridge of the bicipital groove proximally. It causes the same action upon the arm and additionally, provides extension of the humerus when flexed. The coracobrachialis originates at the coracoid process of the scapula, that portion of the scapula that extends frontward, and inserts at the middle of the humerus. It assists with the flexion and adduction of the humerus bone.

Deltoid Muscle

The deltoid is a triangular shaped muscle that provides the rounded shape to the human shoulder. It is further divided into three sections: anterior, middle, and posterior. The main motion of the deltoid is to cause abduction of the arm. The anterior section originates at the outside third of the clavicle. It then inserts at the deltoid tuberosity of the humerus and causes flexion and horizontal rotation of the humerus. The middle deltoid muscle originates at the acromion process of the scapula and inserts also at the deltoid tuberosity. It assists with abduction of the humerus to a 90-degree extension. The posterior deltoid originates at the lower part of the scapula and inserts again at the deltoid tuberosity. It causes the extension, horizontal abduction, and lateral rotation of the humerus.

Supraspinatus, Infraspinatus, and Subscapularis

- Supraspinatus – This muscle originates at the supraspinous fossa of the scapula at the superior portion of this bone. Its insertion point is at the top of the humerus bone. This muscle acts upon the upper arm by instigating abduction in the humerus.
- Infraspinatus – This muscle originates at the infraspinous fossa of the scapula at the medial portion of this bone. It spans a much larger surface area than the supraspinous fossa. This muscle inserts at the greater tubercule, or large round nodule, of the humerus and serves to provide for rotating the humerus laterally.
- Subscapularis – This muscle originates at the back surface of the scapula. This muscle inserts at the lesser tubercle of the humerus. Its function is to provide for rotating the humerus laterally.

Teres Major, the Teres Minor, and the Latissimus Dorsi

The teres major is a thick flat muscle located on the dorsal inferior side of the scapula. The insertion point is the lesser tubercule of the humerus. This muscle extends upward into the tubercule and is responsible for movement of the humerus causing the arm to lower and move in a backward motion. The teres minor is a narrow, long muscle and is considered part of the rotator cuff. The insertion point is the lowest end of the greater tubercule of the humerus. It causes the humerus to move in a backward motion and also to rotate outward. The latissimus dorsi is a large triangular flat muscle located on the posterior side of the body and covers the lumbar region and the last six of the thoracic vertebrae. This muscle extends upwards to insert at the intertubercular groove of the humerus. The actions that are expressed are extension, adduction, and internal rotation of the joint at the shoulder.

Biceps Brachii

The biceps brachii is the muscle located on the anterior upper arm. Its main purpose is to cause the flexion of the arm. The origin of the bicep is at the coracoid process of the scapula (short head) and the glenoid fossa (long head). It then extends down the arm and attaches at the radial tuberosity, a large nodule at the end of the radius. Because of this insertion point, the biceps brachii also has influence on the movement of the forearm. There are three actions caused by this muscle: flexion of the forearm, to extend the arm above the shoulder joint, and to supinate the forearm, that is, to rotate it so the palm faces upwards. The triceps brachii is located on the posterior region of the upper arm. It originates at three points, the infraglenoid tuberosity of the scapula, the proximal half of the humerus, and the distal region of the humerus. The tricep is responsible for extending the elbow. The bicep and tricep work in conjunction as flexors and extensors. The flexor contracts the muscle causing the joint to bend, the extensor then contracts to return the limb to the original position.

Supinator Muscle

The supinator is a wide muscle that curves around the upper third portion of the radius. Its main purpose is to allow the hand and forearm to supinate, or twist so that the palm of the hand faces the body or faces forward. It also uses the bicep brachii muscle to perform this action. The supinator consists of two fibers: the superficial fibers and the upper fibers. This muscle can be difficult to palpate. The pronator teres and the pronator quadratus are two muscles that work together to pronate the hand so that the palm is facing downwards towards the floor. The pronator teres originates at both the humerus and the ulna. It then attaches at the radius. The pronator quadratus runs from both the distal part of the anterior ulna to the distal part of the anterior radius. This muscle assists not only with moving the palm to face downwards, but also to keep the bones of the radius and ulna together.

Muscles That Cause Action

Upper Arm

Approximately eight separate muscles cause action on the upper arm. These muscles are listed below:

- Pectoralis Major (Clavicular and Sternal)
- Coracobrachialis
- Deltoid (Anterior, Middle, and Posterior)
- Supraspinatus
- Infraspinatus
- Subscapularis
- Teres (Minor and Major)
- Latissimus Dorsi

Flexion of the Wrist

The muscles that play a part in causing the action of flexion upon the wrist are:

- Flexor Carpal Radialis – Can be felt on the anterior side of the forearm. It can be palpated on the radial side of the Palmaris longus tendon.
- Flexor Carpal Ulnaris (humeral head and ulnar head) – Located on the proximal half of the forearm.
- Palmaris Longus – Originates from the humerus and inserts at the palmar aponeurosis, also known as the muscles of the palm of the hand.

Extension of the Wrist

The muscles that have a role in creating the action of extension upon the wrist are:

- Extensor Carpi Radialis Longus – Originates at the distal third of the humerus and inserts at the base of the 2nd metacarpal or index finger.
- Extensor Carpi Radialis Brevis – Originates on the lateral side of the humerus and inserts at the base of the 3rd metacarpal, or middle finger.
- Extensor Carpi Ulnaris – Originates on the lateral humerus and inserts at the lateral base of the 5th metacarpal, or pinky finger.

Fingers

The following is a list of the muscles that cause action upon the fingers:

- Flexor Digitorum Superficialis – (includes humeral head, ulnar head, radial and head)
- Flexor Digitorum Profundus
- Flexor Digiti Minimi
- Extensor Digitorum
- Extensor Indicis
- Extensor Digiti Minimi
- Abductor Digiti Minimi
- Opponens Digiti Minimi
- Palmar Interosseous (includes first, second, third, and fourth)
- Dorsal Interosseous
- Lumbricals

Thigh and the Lateral Rotators

The muscles of the lateral rotators and thigh are made up of the gluteus maximum which provides for lateral movement and support of the thigh, the gluteus medius, which abducts the thigh, and the gluteus minimus, which assists with rotating the hip. The internal rotators include the quadratus femoris, the obturator externus and internus, and the gemellus superior and inferior. These muscles aid in rotation of the hip area. Additional muscle groups include the adductor brevis, the adductor longus, and the adductor magnus. These muscles assist with the extension and rotation of the thigh. The psoas major and the illiacus are located in the pelvic region and assist with flexing the thigh and hip and causing the rotation of the knee.

Lower Leg

The posterior thigh region is composed of the biceps femoris, the semi-tendinosus, and the semi-membranosus. These muscles assist with extension of the thigh and rotation of the knee. The biceps femoris is more commonly known as the hamstrings and is made up of two types: long head and short head. The long head of the biceps femoris originates at the ischial tuberosity and the sacrotuberous ligament. It inserts on the lateral side of the fibula and the tibia. The short head originates at the lateral edge of the linea aspera, a rough ridge on the posterior portion of the fibula. Both of these help with lateral rotation of the leg and hip. Other muscles that cause the leg to extend at the knee include the rectus femoris, vastus lateralis, vastus intermedius, and the vastus medialis.

Foot

The following is the list of muscles which act upon the foot and cause moment from inversion, extension, and flexion:

- Popliteus
- Tibialis Anterior
- Peroneus Tertius
- Extensor Digitorum Longus
- Extensor Hallucis Longus
- Gastrocnemius (Medial Head and Lateral Head)
- Plantaris
- Soleus
- Flexor Digitorum Longus
- Flexor Hallucis Longus
- Tibialis Posterior
- Peroneus Longus
- Peroneus Brevis

Abdominal Region

Several muscle groups act upon the abdominal area. These include the rectus abdominis, which is responsible for flexing of the trunk and tensing the abdominal walls. The external obliques run alongside the external surfaces of the lower eight ribs. These muscles extend from below the armpit down towards the waist. They allow for bilateral movement and rotation from side to side of the trunk. The internal obliques lie just underneath the external and provide for the same movements as the external. The transverse abdominis muscles lie underneath the rectus abdominis and also help with flexion and compression of the abdominal wall. The rectus abdominis can be palpitated from the sternum down to the pubis. The external obliques can be felt on the lateral side of the abdomen. The internal obliques and the transverse abdominis are situated deep within the abdominal region and cannot be palpitated.

Respiratory Process

The primary muscle used to assist with the respiratory process is the diaphragm. It is located between the upper lumbar vertebrae, within the region of the six lowest ribs and costal cartilage. The diaphragm has no insertion point. The main purpose of the diaphragm is to contract the muscles used to intake air, or inspiration. The muscle cannot readily be palpitated, but it can be seen during the respiratory process. Other respiratory muscles include the intercostals, made up of the external, internal, and innermost. These muscles are located between each of the ribs and serve to pull apart the ribs during inspiration, allowing for greater lung capacity. The serratus posterior superior, located near the collarbone, and the serratus posterior inferior, located at the base of the ribs, serve to expand the ribs outward and downwards, also leading to an increase in lung capacity.

Spinal Column

The following is the list of the muscles that run alongside the spinal column. All are difficult to palpitate through the skin.

- Quadratus lumborum
- Intertransversarii
- Interspinales
- Rotatores
- Multifidus
- Semispinalis (includes capitis, cervicis, thoracis)
- Spinalis (includes capitis, cervicis, thoracis)
- Longissimus (includes capitis, cervicis, thoracis)

Mastication

Mastication is defined as the act of chewing, or the process by which the teeth break food down into smaller particles that are easily swallowed. Many muscles aid this process. The masseter is responsible for closing the jaw and can be found near the zygomatic arch and the mandible. The temporalis, which originates at the temporal bone, causes the jaw to close and retract. The buccinator, which originates at the maxilla and mandible, helps to keep the cheeks close to the teeth to allow the food to remain in place for chewing. The internal pterygoid helps to close the jaw and allows it to move the jaw from side to side. The external pterygold causes the lower jaw to protrude forwards as in an underbite.

Eye Movement

The muscles of the eye provide for movement from side to side and up and down. They allow a person to focus on objects without moving the head. None of these muscles are able to palpitate. The listing of the eye muscles is as follows:

- Levator palpebrae superioris – Causes the eyelid to open.
- Superior Oblique – Causes the eye to turn out and downwards.
- Supetior Rectus – Causes the eye to rotate upwards.
- Lateral Rectus – Causes lateral movement.
- Inferior Rectus – Moves the eye downwards.
- Medial Rectus – Moves the eye medially.
- Inferior Oblique – Moves the eye upwards and out.

Expressions

The muscles that show expressions of happiness, sadness, anger, etc. are aided by the following muscle groups:

- Epicranius
- Corrugator
- Procerus
- Orbicularis Oculi
- Nasalis
- Dialator Naris
- Quadratus Labii Superioris
- Zygomaticus
- Obicularis Oris

- Risorius
- Depressor Anguli Oris
- Depressor Labii Inferioris
- Mentalis
- Platysma
- Auricularis

Forehead Region

The muscle groups that assist the body with creating movements such as frowning, drawing the eyebrows together, wrinkling the forehead, and drawing the nose upwards are listed below:

- Epicranius (consisting of the occipitalis and frontalis) – this muscle originates just above the occipital ridge and inserts at the epicranial aponeurosis. The action this muscle performs is to draw the epicranius towards the back, or posterior, of the head, and to raise the eyebrows, causing the forehead to wrinkle. This muscle is sometimes known as the occipitofrontalis.
- Corrugator – This muscle is also known as the corrugator supercilli. It is triangular in shape and is responsible for the action of wrinkling the forehead and frowning.
- Procerus – The origin of this muscle is within the fascia located over the cartilage in the nasal area. It inserts between the eyebrows and deep within the skin. This muscle is responsible for the action of wrinkling the nose.

Eye and the Nostrils

The muscles that are involved with this region of the face include:

- Orbicularis Oculi – Controls the opening and closing of the eye. This muscle originates at the nasal bone and circles the eyeball. The insertion point of this muscle is all around the eye as the muscles blend in with the surrounding areas.
- Nasalis – This muscle originates above the incisors at the maxilla bone. It then blends in with the procerus muscle. The purpose of this muscle is to compress the bridge of the nostrils, and allow the external area of the nostrils to elevate, or flare, and also to depress the tip of the nose.
- Dialator Naris – This muscle allows the nostril opening to expand. It originates at the greater alar cartridge and inserts at the end point of the nose.

Mouth

The muscles that involve movement to the mouth include:

- Quadratus Labii Superioris –Lies next to the nose and extends to the zygomatic arch: Raising or elevating the upper lip.
- Zygomaticus (major and minor) –Located from one side of the zygomatic arch to the corner of the mouth. Contraction causes the mouth to draw back and upwards, as in the case of smiling.
- Obicularis Oris –Originates from muscles around the mouth and inserts at the lips; circular in nature, allows the mouth to remain closed, aids in chewing, speech, and facial expression.
- Risorius –Originates over the masseter; inserts at the muscle surrounding the mouth and at corners of the mouth, brings the mouth backwards at an angle.
- Depressor Anguli Oris – This muscle draws the mouth into a downward position and is located at the outer edge of the chin.
- Depressor Labii Inferioris – Helps to depress the lower lip.

- Mentalis – This muscle causes the chin to rise up and also enables a person to pout.
- Platysma – This muscle causes the mouth to draw in a downward direction as when making an expression of sadness. It also causes the skin of the neck to wrinkle.

CIRCULATORY SYSTEM

The circulatory system is also known as the vascular system. Vascular is defined as a vessel that is made up of a tube-like structure. These vessels help to transport fluids such as blood, or lymph within the body of an organism. The circulatory system is responsible for controlling the circulation within an organism through the removal of waste products and by providing essential nutrients to tissues. There are two divisions within the circulatory system. The first is the blood-vascular system also known as the cardiovascular system. It includes all the vessels used to transport blood such as the veins, arteries, capillaries, and also the heart. The second division is known as the lymph-vascular system or lymphatic system. It includes the lymphoid organs, lymph nodes, lymph ducts, and the lymphatic vessels that are used to transport lymph from the tissues to the circulatory system.

HEART

The heart is part of the cardiovascular system, which also consists of the blood vessels, capillaries, veins, and the blood itself. The heart is a four-chambered muscle whose sole function is to pump oxygen rich blood throughout the body. The heart is composed of the left atrium, right atrium, left ventricle, and right ventricle. The atria are the chambers located superior to the ventricles. The pathway that blood takes through the heart is cyclical, meaning that the path that the blood follows is through a closed system. The veins carry the blood from the rest of the body to the heart, and enter at the right atrium. From there, it flows into the right ventricle. After it leaves the right ventricle, it travels past the pulmonary valve to enter the lungs. Here, the blood disposes of the wastes from the body and gathers a fresh supply of oxygen from the lungs and then reenters through the left atrium. From here, the blood travels to the left ventricle where the aorta helps to propel the oxygen rich blood to the rest of the body.

ARTERIES, CAPILLARIES, AND VEINS

The arteries, capillaries, and veins are tube-like structures that are responsible for the transportation of blood, lymph, and other substances throughout the body. The arteries are defined as those vessels that carry blood away from the heart. These help to carry fresh oxygen-rich blood and other nutrients from the heart to other parts of the body. The veins carry blood, waste products, and carbon dioxide from the organs to the heart. Vein walls are thinner and less muscular than arteries. Veins also contain valves which prevent the backwards flow of blood. Capillaries are defined as those blood vessels that are microscopic in size and form a network connecting arterioles and venules. With capillaries being one cell layer thick, it is a simple process for wastes to pass readily into capillaries and for oxygenated nutritive rich blood to enter into organs. Capillaries function as the network by which arterioles and venules connect. They are thin-walled and have a high degree of permeability. Diffusion is the process whereby a substance flows from an area that is higher in density to one that is lower. Capillaries carrying oxygen-rich blood filled with nutrients are denser than the tissues surrounding the capillary. The area within the tissues is filled with cellular waste and carbon dioxide. As the transfer occurs, the nutrients diffuse into the tissues while the wastes diffuse into the capillaries to then be transported back to the heart. The wastes and carbon dioxide are released into the lungs for removal from the body and the blood is then filled with fresh oxygenated blood. Filtration is the process by which the blood pressure forces the nutrients into the tissues and also forces the wastes from the tissues into the capillaries. This is easily accomplished as a result of the thinness of the capillary walls.

RED AND WHITE BLOOD CELLS

Red blood cells are the mechanism by which nutrients and oxygen are delivered to the body's tissues. Red blood cells are shaped like semi-flat circular discs. They have the ability to distort their shape to maneuver through small channels. Certain diseases of the blood are caused by physiological changes to the red blood cells or by lack of sufficient numbers of red blood cells within the body. They are also known as erythrocytes. White blood cells are made within the bone marrow and assist with helping the body's immune system fight off illnesses and injuries. An overproduction of white blood cells in the body can indicate a disease requiring further testing. One example would be leukemia. White blood cells help fight infection by encircling bacteria or by producing antibodies to help stave off an infection. They are also known as leukocytes.

LYMPHATIC SYSTEM

The lymphatic system is also known as the lymph-vascular system. Lymph is made up of primarily white blood cells and is liquid in form. Its makeup is similar to the interstitial fluid of the surrounding tissues and it helps with the exchange of waste materials and nutrients from the tissues to the cells. Approximately 90% of the fluid is able to pass through the capillary walls and renter the blood stream for the return to the heart; however, the last 10% contains particles that are too large to pass through these walls. Lymph fluid then collects these to transport to the lymphatic ducts and then ultimately return to the blood. Lymphatic massage has many benefits upon the body including helping expel wastes from the lymph nodes and also to increase circulation. It also helps to clean tissues and aid in the production of lymphocytes to increase the body's immune system response.

LYMPH NODES

There are approximately 500-600 lymph nodes ranging up to about an inch in length located in all areas of the body. Specifically they can be found in the following regions:

- At the back of the head – Assists with drainage of wastes from the scalp area.
- Back and sides of the neck – Assists with drainage of mouth and nasal cavities
- Under the jaw – Helps to drain the mouth.
- Along the upper extremities – Located under the armpit, in the crook of the elbow, and under the chest muscle.
- Abdominal region – Lymph nodes are located along the blood vessels in this area.
- Lower extremities – Located in the groin and at the back of the knee.

IMMUNE SYSTEM

The immune system is responsible for protecting the body from outside influences such as bacteria, toxins, and viruses. It also accounts for the response to any internal changes to the body such as the development of cancerous cells and tumors and also any illnesses resulting to damage to the organs or tissues. The response of the immune system is to create an antibody that works against the antigen or "antibody-generating" substance to render it inactive. Once an antigen is discovered in the body, the immune system creates antibody proteins that bind to the antigen and then diminish its control over the body. There are two types of immunity. Innate immunity is present at birth and the degree to which the immunity is present depends on the amount of immunity derived from the mother. The second type of immunity is acquired immunity. This form usually refers to the immunity obtained as a result of a vaccination. Immunity garnered in this fashion can last from days or weeks to even years, depending on the bacteria or virus being vaccinated against.

Review Video: Immune System
Visit mometrix.com/academy and enter code: 622899

Repair Process

When a person's body exhibits anything besides a healthy condition, the immune system starts to work on the repair process. The cells release proteins such as histamines and cytokines to begin the process of healing. This release corresponds with the constriction of blood vessels to help prevent excessive bleeding. Following this, the capillaries then dilate to allow for the influx of white blood cells and antibodies to fill the injured area. Platelets and fibrin step in to help stop any bleeding which may have occurred and also to stop any potentially harmful matter from entering the blood. They also begin the process clotting to stop the bleeding. Any pathogens are inactivated by neutrophils and macrophages, and finally, collagen enters the area to repair and mend any damaged tissues by creating scar tissue. At this point, any inflammation will have begun to subside within 72 hours. Scar tissue may continue to be produced for weeks or months depending upon the severity of the injury. When inflammation is present, massage is contraindicated as it impedes the healing process. However, after the swelling has decreased, massage is helpful to stimulate the production of scar tissue.

Dysfunctions

- Allergies –Immune system reacts to a substance normally deemed harmless; stimulants: dust, mold, pet dander, pollen, fungus, or food (wheat, dairy, peanuts, or eggs); reaction: can be coughing, itching, sneezing, rashes, respiratory distress, etc.
- Autoimmune diseases – ex: rheumatoid arthritis and multiple sclerosis; body attacks its own tissues and cells; causes fatigue, joint swelling, vision problems, and weakness.
- Cancer – Occurs when the body rapidly produces an abnormal amount of cellular growth within an area. Cancers affecting the immune system include leukemia, multiple myeloma, and lymphoma. Leukemia affects the body's immune system by the overproduction of white blood cells. Multiple myeloma is a type of blood cancer in which there is an overproduction of plasma cells causing tumors in bone marrow throughout the body. Lymphoma is also a cancer of the blood whereby the lymphocytes either reproduce in greater quantities than needed or remain in the blood longer than necessary. May show up in the blood, bone marrow, the lymph nodes, spleen, or other organs.

Infection vs. Inflammation

An infection within the body is an indication of the presence of microorganisms such as bacteria, fungi, parasites, and viruses, capable of causing harm to the body. These microorganisms generally enter the body through cuts in the skin, through nasal passages, or from shared bodily fluids. The damage they cause can range from simple localized illnesses to a disease that ravages the entire body. Local infections are those that affect one small area of the body. If the infection has spread to other areas or all over the body, then it is termed a systemic infection. It is important that massage techniques are not performed on localized cases of infection or on the entire body in cases of systemic infections. Inflammation can result from an infection and causes five major changes to the body: redness, heat, swelling, pain, and loss of all or portions of the function of the affected body part. Inflammation indicates tissue damage and is the result of inflow of blood to the area as well as an increase in the production of white blood cells to aid in the healing process. It is important that these areas are not massaged while inflammation is present or while the patient exhibits fever.

Nervous System

The nervous system is composed of the various muscle groups that are responsible for coordination of the body's activities, provides monitoring of the organs of the body, and allows the nerves to sense or perceive feeling and touch from all areas of the body. The main components of the nervous system include the brain, spinal cord, and the nerves. The brain sends the electrical impulses by way of the spinal cord to reach nerve endings through the body. These impulses control movement, sensation, feelings, and even thought. The nervous system controls the way that our body perceives input whether from internal or external sources. Additionally, nervous system movement can be either intentional or unintentional. The nervous system provides an organism with the ability to process the senses of sight, hearing, tasting, smell, touch, and also to function cognitively as in moving, talking, and thinking.

Brain

The brain is composed of three segments: the cerebrum, cerebellum, and the medulla, which all interact with different parts of the nervous system. The cerebrum is located on the superior portion of the brain and is divided into the left and right hemispheres. The cerebrum is the largest section of the brain and provides for both motor and sensory processes. The cerebrum is the area where higher learning thought processes take place. The cerebellum is located inferior to the cerebrum yet just above the brain stem. The cerebellum is responsible for the motor and sensory actions also and can assist with maintaining one's balance and posture. The cerebellum affects one's attention span and ability to process language and music. The cerebellum is also divided into two hemispheres. The medulla oblongata is the lowest part of the brain stem. It resides inferior to the cerebellum and superior to the spinal cord. The focus of the medulla oblongata is to control the body's autonomic functions to include respiration, digestion, excretion, and cardiovascular functioning.

Pain vs. Stress

Pain causes a sensation ranging from slight to severe that indicates potential damage to the tissues or possible destruction within the body. Pain can be an indicator of damage from the nerve endings that lie beneath the surface of the skin, damage to the periosteum of the bones, damage to blood vessels and arteries, and finally, deeper damage to internal organs and muscles. The body's response to pain is both physical and physiological. By this, it is meant that the response to pain mimics the same reaction that the body experiences as a result from stress. Stress is any condition that causes strain on the body or tension within the body. It can affect the internal balance and harmony within the body. Stress affects each person differently at varying levels. Overall, increased stress can be detrimental to the health of the individual. The body's reaction to stress is indicated by increased heart rate, secretion of "fight or flight" hormones from the adrenal gland, deeper breathing, and increased blood pressure.

Endocrine System

The hormone producing glands that make up the endocrine system are listed as follows:

- Hypothalamus
- Pineal Gland
- Pituitary Gland (Anterior & Posterior)
- Thyroid Gland
- Parathyroid Gland
- Heart
- Stomach & Intestines

- Liver
- Islets of Langerhans in the Pancreas
- Adrenal Glands (Adrenal Cortex and Adrenal Medulla)
- Kidney
- Skin
- Adipose Tissue
- Testes – Males only
- Ovarian follicle – Females only
- Corpus Luteum – Females only
- Placenta – Females only during pregnancy

Review Video: Endocrine System
Visit mometrix.com/academy and enter code: 678939

Hormones

Hormones are those chemical substances produced by the endocrine glands that cause actions on tissues or organs within the body. Hormones can lead to an increase in growth, can activate the immune system process, and can bring about the onset of changes such as puberty or menopause. Hormones are also responsible for initiating the fight or flight response to fear or other stimuli such as stress. The body's metabolism is also regulated by hormonal changes. In addition, the release of hormones can help a woman's body with maintaining and carrying a fetus to term and also can help with aftercare. The production of hormones can be caused by the release of other hormones, by environmental factors, or by activity generating from the brain. Overall, hormones play a key role in the metabolic process enabling the body to function.

Reproductive System

The reproductive system consists of those organs and hormones that deal specifically with reproduction of the same type of organism. In humans and multi-celled organisms, this process is achieved sexually with both a male and a female organism. In one-celled organisms, the process is called non-sexual or asexual reproduction, as they do not require a partner in order to reproduce. In the human male, the purpose of the reproductive organs is to produce sperm, release male hormones, and perform the act necessary for reproduction. The male sexual organs include the penis, testes, vas deferens, prostate glands, seminal vesicles, and the bulbourethral glands. In the human female, the purpose of the reproductive organs is to provide for the development of the growing fetus after being impregnated by the male sperm. The organs involved in the female reproductive system include the ovaries, fallopian tubes, uterus, vagina, and the external genitalia.

Review Video: Reproductive Systems
Visit mometrix.com/academy and enter code: 505450

Respiration

Respiration is the process by which the body exchanges carbon dioxide wastes from the body for fresh oxygen. This gaseous exchange occurs in three separate areas.

- Inside the lungs, blood carries the carbon dioxide wastes to exchange with the oxygen from the external environment.
- The internal respiration process is completed when the blood carries fresh oxygen to tissue cells throughout the body and then makes the transfer.
- Respiration also occurs within the individualized cells.

Respiration begins with the intake of oxygen through the nasal passages where it is carried down through the trachea, becoming moistened and filtered along the way. Once in the bronchi, it divides into the smaller bronchial trees and moves further in until it ends at the alveoli, a tiny cluster of air sacs signifying the end of the air passages. Tiny capillaries and arteries surround the alveoli. Through the process of diffusion, the carbon dioxide and oxygen are exchanged, thus allowing the oxygen to enter the bloodstream where it is then carried away throughout the body, and the carbon dioxide is then exhaled back into the environment.

Review Video: Respiratory System
Visit mometrix.com/academy and enter code: 783075

Common Disorders

Causes of disorders: genetic or environmental. Examples: pollution, smog, smoking toxic chemicals, etc. A healthy respiratory system needs clean air, deep breathing exercises, a healthy diet, and regular exercise to maintain optimal health. The **common cold** is readily transmitted through physical contact and is caused by many viruses. **Influenza** is also highly contagious and can be spread through the air as well as on surfaces. **Pneumonia** is a more serious condition resulting in inflammation of the lungs and increased mucus production as the lungs work to stave off viruses and bacteria. **Bronchitis** can be a chronic condition in which the bronchial tubes are inflamed and produce copious amounts of mucus. **Asthma** is a condition resulting in excessive coughing and wheezing that can be exacerbated by cold air, dust, dander, etc. **Sinusitis** affects the swelling of the nasal cavities usually as the result of allergens, obstructions, or infections. **Tuberculosis** is a highly contagious bacterial airborne disease that causes devastating effects on a person with a compromised immune system.

Digestive Process

The purpose of the digestive system is to digest food and also to absorb it for use by the body's tissues and organs for energy. The digestive system is made up of the alimentary canal and also the accessory digestive organs. The alimentary canal is the gastrointestinal tract and is made up of the following organs or parts of the body: mouth, pharynx, esophagus, stomach, small intestine, and large intestine. The accessory digestive organs are those that greatly assist with the digestive process, but play a secondary role. For example, the teeth, tongue, salivary glands, liver, pancreas, and gallbladder all aid in digestion but are parts of the body that can be eliminated and still the body can do function in processing food. The process of digestion begins in the mouth where the teeth aid in breaking down the particles into manageable pieces. After mastication, saliva helps to propel food down the esophagus and into the stomach. Acids break down the food further and then the food leaves to enter the small intestine. Here, the food is broken down further and absorbed by the villi, small projections that line the small intestine. After this point, waste products are moved into the large intestine where they are prepared for expulsion from the body through the rectum.

Review Video: Gastrointestinal System
Visit mometrix.com/academy and enter code: 378740

Excretory System

The excretory system is the system by which waste products are removed from the body. Since this system does not only include wastes from food absorption, it also can refer to respiratory wastes, such as carbon dioxide or wastes excreted in the process of sweating. The organs involved in the excretory system are the kidneys, sweat glands, lungs and the rectum. If these wastes are not excreted yet remain within the body, they can cause serious health problems for the individual. The urinary system is composed of the kidneys, bladder, ureter, hilum, and the urethra. As the body absorbs nutrients, wastes are sent to the kidneys for processing. From here it travels to the bladder where it is released from the body through the urethra. Visual changes to the color of the urine or in the measured amount released from the body can indicate damage elsewhere in the body. Urine can be tested for the presence of drugs, white blood cells, blood, glucose, and hormonal imbalances and is therefore a good indicator of the body's overall health.

Massage Benefits and Contraindications

PHYSIOLOGICAL EFFECTS

Western massage, otherwise known as Swedish massage, helps to relax the body, increase metabolism, speed healing, and provide emotional and physical relaxation. Similar massages on two individuals can produce two entirely different reactions. Techniques used in Swedish massage include light touches and gentle stimulation over the skin, producing reflexive sensations. Mechanical stimulation of the body with increased pressure on the muscles and tissues results in an increase in blood flow to the area causing an increase in nutrients and oxygen, and removal of wastes from the muscle. The effects of muscles on the body at the end of the massage session are a relaxed state, increase in flexibility and a decrease in pain. An increase in the production of sweat and oil from the glands can be seen at the end of the massage. There is an improvement in blood flow to the area resulting in a temporary color change in the skin. Finally, the skin temperature becomes warmer, and the skin exhibits an increase in suppleness.

MUSCULAR EFFECTS

When a massage is being performed, the muscles undergo a transformation that helps them increase the nutritional intake, improve circulation, and helps to stimulate cellular activity within the muscle. Massage relaxes tense muscles and helps to alleviate the pain associated with muscle spasms. During a massage, blood passes through the muscular tissue at a rate three times more than when the muscle is at rest. This action brings new supplies of blood to the area and assists with the removal of waste material. After strenuous exercise, massage helps to alleviate the pain, stiffness, and soreness associated with the exercise. If massage is prescribed as a therapy after an injury, the muscle experiences less scarring and buildup of connective tissue. Range of motion is also increased through massage and circulation is increased that also helps to reduce the time off due to the injury.

NERVOUS SYSTEM EFFECTS

The nervous system is comprised of the central nervous system, made up of the brain and spinal cord, and the peripheral nervous system, made up of the autonomic nervous system, cranial nerves, and spinal nerves. The nervous system has the ability to be both stimulated and soothed depending upon the type of muscle massages being utilized. Techniques that stimulate the body include friction, percussion, and vibration. Light rubbing, rolling or wringing of the skin is known as the technique of friction. Percussion involves a series of tapping to increase the nervous irritability. Depending on the duration, percussion has the ability to numb the nerves within the area. Vibration involves shaking or trembling movements upon the body part. The end result is to stimulate peripheral nerves. Soothing techniques that produce a calming effect include light stroking upon the skin, and petrissage, which are light kneading movements on the skin. Putting pressure on a specific trigger point desensitizes the area and releases hypertension in the muscle.

The autonomic nervous system is divided into two distinct areas: the sympathetic nervous system and the parasympathetic nervous system. The sympathetic nervous system is responsible for the "fight or flight" response, while the parasympathetic system counters these effects and helps to return the body to a relaxed state by reducing the heart rate and increasing circulation to bring about a relaxed state of being. The sympathetic nervous system, by contrast, increases the alertness of the body through the release of adrenaline and epinephrine. When a massage is performed, the reaction from the autonomic nervous system is one of initial invigoration, and after a short time period has passed, becomes one of relaxation and sedation. The parasympathetic nervous system is stimulated leading to a reduction in epinephrine and norepinephrine and lowering of blood pressure.

Circulatory System Effects

When techniques such as massage, pressure, stroking, and percussion are performed upon the body, the circulatory system responds in a favorable manner leading to benefits throughout the body. Stroking the skin lightly causes dilation in the capillaries. Applying stronger pressure while stroking also leads to a flushed look to the skin and also a longer lasting period of dilation. Percussion of the muscles leads to a contraction of the blood vessels that gradually eases up and causes a relaxed state. Applying friction to the muscle and skin produces a rapid response of blood to flow through the veins. It also accounts for the flow of interstitial fluid to increase leading to a healthy cellular environment. Kneading the muscles causes the blood to flow into the deeper sections of arteries and veins. Lighter massage techniques are responsible for lymph circulation and ease the tendency towards edema in these areas. Compression causes muscles to store a larger quantity of blood. Finally, all massage techniques should be directed towards the heart: from the ends of the appendages towards the torso, and also from the head downward.

Dopamine and Serotonin

During a massage, chemicals are released within the body that provides positive physiological effects upon the body. Neurochemicals such as dopamine and serotonin are released that contribute to pain control and an elevation in one's mood. One neurotransmitter is dopamine which helps to control the brain's emotions, motor skills, and feelings of pleasure or pain. Serotonin is another type of neurotransmitter that also helps regulate moods, behavior, appetite, and memory. Low levels of serotonin can contribute to depression, anxiety, sleep disorders, and even personality disorders. Massage helps to increase the levels of these neurotransmitters within the body and lead to a sense of peacefulness and calmness that can help to reduce stress. They also help contribute to appetite control and increased function of the immune system.

Pain Management

Pain management is one of the benefits obtained through massage therapy as the muscle receives an influx of blood circulating through the tissue. Through a process known as gate control theory, the transmission of pain sensation is interrupted from the affected area and prevented from reaching the central nervous system. This is accomplished through stimulation of cutaneous receptors. Massage techniques such as rubbing and applying pressure also suppresses the pain sensation from reaching the receptors in the brain. An example of this is the response of rubbing an area that has been struck, helping to minimize the degree of pain felt.

Contraindications

When performing a massage on a new client, it is important that the therapist obtain as thorough a medical history as possible. A contraindication is any procedure or treatment plan that is not advisable for the benefit and well being of the patient. There are three types of contraindications that can exist: absolute, regional, or conditional. An absolute contraindication indicates that a massage should not be performed under any circumstances. Examples of this would include shock, pneumonia or pregnancy related toxemia. A regional contraindication would exist when a client cannot have massage performed on a specific region of the body due to injuries such as open wounds, a contagious condition that could cause harm to the therapist, or arthritis that would result in creating additional pain to the client if the areas were massaged. A final contraindication is conditional. This means that the massage therapist must make accommodations in the therapeutic plan to help the client obtain the most benefit from the massage while avoiding the areas that could cause discomfort.

The following can be contraindications to a massage due to the potential for hurting a client:

- Active high body temperature
- Infectious disease (influenza, colds, etc.)
- Inflammation (of a body appendage or a joint)
- Osteoporosis
- Varicose Veins
- Hematoma or Contusion (bruise, mild to severe)
- Edema
- High Blood Pressure
- Acne
- Cancer
- Rashes
- Hernia
- Tumors or Warts

This list is not all inclusive, however, it is important to work with the client on acknowledging all potentially dangerous conditions without the consent of the client's physician.

PREGNANCY

During the normal pregnancy, the mother can benefit from a massage to aid in decreasing the discomfort and aches associated with back pain, leg pain, stress, and fatigue as a result of the pregnancy. In order to provide the best care for the mother, it is important to note the mother's condition and absolutely avoid massage when there is a risk of toxemia or pre-eclampsia. The accompanying high blood pressure, edema, nausea, and diarrhea do not bode well with a massage and can inflict harm to the mother. To prep the client, the massage therapist must ensure that both the mother and unborn child are in a comfortable position on the table, preferably facing up and in a semi-reclined position. When the client is lying on her side, it is important to place pillows under the head and between the knees to help support the back. Avoidance of massage in the abdominal area is indicated and during the latter part of the pregnancy also, the therapist should not have the mother lay prone on her abdomen.

CANCER

When performing a massage, the utmost importance is placed on the client's well being. As such, the therapist should be aware of the contraindications of a cancer patient.

A complete medical history should be taken with the consultation from the physician or oncologist to determine if it would be recommended as a form of treatment.

Factors to seek out are:

- Location of cancer and type
- The stage of the cancer
- Additional sites for metastasis
- The treatment level of the cancer
- Immune system condition for the person at the time of the massage
- The stamina level and attitude of the person

During the actual massage, light or moderate pressure should be used and avoidance of deep massage over areas where tumors are known to exist.

Massage Preparation

Set-up

Depending on the extent of the practice and the funds available, the therapist should have basic equipment for the following areas of the practice: the office area, the massage area, and the restroom facility or the hydrotherapy area. A smaller independent massage therapist will generally work out of the home or in a small office. The business area should be cordoned off from client access for confidentiality purposes and allow for privacy for client consultations. The restroom facility provides a place for clients to shower before and after the massage and to provide an area for the massage therapist to wash hands between each client's massage. Finally, the massage area is made up of the massage table, a stool, an area for storage of linens, oils, creams, etc. and a dressing area for the client. Pillows or bolsters should be readily available to help make the client more comfortable during the massage. Appropriate drapes should be located nearby for privacy of the patient during the massage.

Relaxation

The ideal size for a typical massage room should be no less than 10 feet wide by 12 feet long in order to accommodate the size of the massage table, desk, and storage areas for linens and lotions, while also providing enough space for the therapist to adequately maneuver around the table to perform the massage. Considering that the client will not have clothes on during the massage, it is important to have an ideal temperature in the room to prevent chills. A temperature of 72° Fahrenheit would ensure the comfort of the client as well as the therapist who may become overheated while performing the massage. Proper ventilation should also be in place to provide fresh air free from odors. The lighting within the room should not be harsh and glaring, and instead should use reflective or soft lighting to make the client feel comfortable. The use of dimmer switches to adjust lighting depending on the client's needs would be a simple investment. Music also helps bring about relaxation; however, it is best to select music based on the client's preferences rather than the therapist's.

Massage Table

Next to the massage therapist's hands, a massage table is one of the most important pieces of equipment. It should be determined whether the table be used in a home setting or in an office environment. The table should be firm and stable for the client's use and also comfortable. To measure for the correct height, the therapist should choose a table that enables him to place his hands flat on the surface while still allowing the arms to remain straight. This yields the best height to provide leverage and to aid in prevention of fatigue of the back, neck, shoulders, and arms while performing the massage. Tables are also made with hydraulic or manual height adjustments that are especially useful if different therapists will be using the same table. The standard size of a massage table is approximately 29 inches wide and 68 to 72 inches long, to account for the average client size, however, this may be too short for a taller individual. Padding on the table should be at least one to two inches of high-density foam for optimal comfort for the client. A vinyl covering is preferred over any other type of covering due to ease of cleaning and sanitizing between clients. To care for the vinyl, a solution of mild detergent is all that is needed. Some massage tables are also adjustable to accommodate patient needs.

Contamination

To maintain the clientele, a therapist must have a facility that is clean and sterile, and practice sanitary procedures in order to protect against the spread of disease and safeguard the well being of the clients. Following strict laws regulating sanitation procedures, the massage therapist must utilize disinfectants, antiseptics and other cleaning agents to maintain a healthy environment. Illness and disease-causing pathogens are transmitted from one infected person to another either directly or indirectly. They can enter the body through inhalation, ingestion, through broken skin, contact with mucous membranes, or through sexual contact. Other pathogens can be transmitted through beverages or food. Types of pathogens the massage therapist may be concerned about are bacteria, fungus, and viruses. Bacteria are most common on dirty surfaces and in unclean water and can cause illnesses such as pneumonia, typhoid fever, TB, diphtheria and syphilis, to name a few. Viruses can invade living hosts and can transmit diseases such as colds, mumps, measles, and pneumonia. Warm, moist environments create an ideal area for fungi and mold to reproduce. Fungal infections are responsible for ringworm, athlete's foot, and Candida.

Safe Environment

The following steps are considered as a precaution to stop the spread of infection:

- Washing hands with soap and water before contact and after contact with each client. Using disposable paper towels rather than cloth.
- Washing skin and hands thoroughly if any contact is made with contaminated fluids.
- Wearing of gloves when performing certain tasks and washing hands after removing the gloves.
- Washing linens contaminated with blood or bodily fluids in hot water with bleach and dried in a hot dryer.
- Handling contaminated linens as little as possible and separating them from other linens.
- Cleaning of surfaces such as walls and ceilings with disinfectant if they come in contact with spills requiring sanitation.

Initial Consultation

From the initial meeting between the client and the massage therapist information is given on both sides to help the client achieve results from the massage therapy. The therapist should greet the client and try to set a positive tone from the onset. The therapist should provide information regarding policies and procedures such as the types of services offered, explanation of the educational background and credentials of the therapist, business practices, listing of the fees for services, and description of a common massage session. The client, in turn, can provide information regarding the medical background, any other illnesses or diseases that can be a contraindication to massage therapy, and consent to treatment. The client and therapist should come to an agreement on the plan of treatment with feedback on both sides after an assessment is taken to determine specific areas needing attention through therapy. Finally, an opportunity should be provided for the client to ask questions of the therapist and also sign an informed consent, thus agreeing to be treated.

Massage Techniques

Basic Massage Movements

The basic massage movements are as follows:

1. Touch – to include superficial or deep massage
2. Gliding or effleurage movements – moving the hand or forearm over the body with varying amounts of pressure being applied. Can be aura stroking, superficial or deep.
3. Kneading – Includes petrissage, rolling of the skin, lifting, and squeezing.
4. Friction – Causing one layer of skin tissue to rub against another. Can be performed by rolling, compression, wringing, and vibration.
5. Percussion – alternately striking the surface of the skin through cupping, slapping, tapping, and beating.
6. Joint movements – manipulating the limbs of the body through passive or active movements.

Touch

Touch is defined as the action of making skin-to-skin contact between the massage therapist's hand and the client's body. Touch is the absence of movement. The pressure can range from extremely light to deep pressure depending on the type of reaction the therapist is trying to achieve. Touch can have a calming physiological effect on the client. The massage therapist should open the massage session with a few moments of touch as a means of connecting with the client and becoming comfortable with his personal body space. This time of gentle touch is also performed at the end of the massage to signal the end of the session and also to provide a sense of closure for both the client and the therapist. Deep pressure can also be applied through touch. In this sense, touch is applied to calm, anesthetize, or stimulate the muscles. It is often used to soothe muscle spasms or alleviate pain. The force is applied through body movement rather than solely relying upon the strength in the arms of the therapist.

Gliding

The types of movements that are based on maneuvering the hand over the client's body with varying degrees of pressure are known as gliding. Ethereal or aura stroking is the process by which the practitioner glides his hands over the length of the client's body without actually touching the body. The intent behind this gesture is to smooth over the energy field that surrounds the body according to some philosophies. A second type of gliding movement is called feather stroking in which long gentle strokes are performed from the center of the body outward. Effleurage is a common Swedish massage technique that calls for successive stokes over a long surface of the body. The pressure subsequently increases with each stroke. Superficial gliding involves applying light pressure to the body from the hand over all surfaces. This gives the therapist a chance to assess the muscle condition prior to commencing the massage. Deep gliding strokes are performed based upon three factors: the amount of pressure exerted, the part of the hand that is used, and the way that the pressure is applied. Deep gliding strokes are designed to stretch and broaden the muscle tissue and fascia. It is best to make these movements towards the heart to encourage blood and lymph flow.

Petrissage

Kneading, or petrissage, is used on the fleshy parts of the body to bring about movement of fluid in deep tissues and help stretch the muscle tissue. The skin is generally raised between the hands and kneaded with firm pressure in circular motions, oftentimes using both hands to perform this motion. A type of petrissage is known as fulling in which the tissue is lifted up and then spread out to enhance the area in between the muscular tissue. Another form of petrissage is called skin rolling. In this method, the fingers pick up the skin in alternate motions and gently pull it away from the underlying tissues to create a stretching of the fascia. This motion warms the skin and helps to remove any buildup of adhesions on the tissue.

Friction

Friction helps to move the superficial layers of tissue against the deeper tissues within the body. The action of friction causes warmth when the therapist presses tissue upon tissue, thereby flattening it, releasing fluids from the tissue, and also stretching it at the same time. The warmth produced also causes the client's metabolic rate to increase. Types of friction methods include circular friction and cross-fiber friction. As the name indicates, circular friction involves the movement of the fingers or hands over the client in a circular pattern. Cross-fiber friction is performed at a sharp transverse direction to the muscle being worked on. This is the preferred method used in rehabilitation of a specific muscle group and promotes the rebuilding of elastic tissue fibers.

Friction techniques

- Compression is the rhythmic movement of the hands or fingers onto the muscular tissue. Palmar compression is directed onto the muscles transverse from the bone. It does not require the use of oils or lotions in performing this technique and in fact, can be performed over clothing. It is commonly used in sports massage.
- Rolling is the method in which a body part is rapidly passed back and forth between the hands. This encourages warmth and relation of the deeper muscle tissue.
- Chucking is the process by which the tissue is grabbed between the hands and moving the tissue up and down the length of the bone. This method is performed rather quickly.
- Wringing is the process similar to wringing water from a towel. The hands work in opposing directions as the flesh is twisted against the bone.
- Vibration is the movement used either manually or in conjunction with a device that produces continuous trembling movements against the muscle. This action helps to desensitize and numb the area.

Percussion

Percussion movements are made up of quick striking motions that are made alternately against the body. This technique serves to stimulate the body, yet each movement does not apply great force. The types of percussion are slapping, tapping, cupping, hacking and beating. Slapping involves applying pressure from the flat palm of the hand against the surface of the body. Tapping uses the fingertips in such a way as only the pads of the fingers come in contact with the body. The fingers can be either held in a flexed position or straight. Either way, the pressure applied is very light. Cupping involves the shaping of the hand into a curved shape prior to being applied to the body. This method is generally performed in the rib area and is a common technique used by respiratory therapists to eliminate build up of lung congestion. Hacking is the use of the ulnar side of the hands to strike against the body, causing an improvement in circulation and relaxation. Beating uses loose fists to gently pound against the body and is considered the heaviest and deepest form of percussion. This is used primarily in the dense muscle tissue.

Joint movements

One type of joint movement is known as passive joint movement. It is generally performed when the client is in a relaxed state and the therapist is able to maneuver, exercise, and stretch a part of the body. PJM is also used to determine the extent of any injuries to the client and also to determine the exact range of motion that part of the body can achieve. Working the muscle and joint in this way allows the therapist to help improve the mobility of the joint and extend the range of motion. To perform the passive joint movement, the therapist must take care in moving the limb only in the direction that the limb is designed to move without any forceful or sharp gestures. If the movement is to assess damage, then stopping at the point of the client's pain is indicated. To rehabilitate the joint, further extension of the limb is recommended.

In active joint movement, the client is responsible for contracting the muscle to perform the required movement of the joint. It is commonly used as an assessment tool to determine the exact capabilities of the range of motion of the client. The results can be benchmarked at the start of treatment with a comparison made at the end of treatment to note the progress made. Active assistive joint movement is performed when the client attempts to move the joint through a series of movements. The therapist assists when the client no longer has the strength or ability to move the injured limb further. This is primarily a therapeutic device designed to restore mobility in the limb. Another type of joint movement is active resistive joint movement. In this action, the therapist or practitioner applies resistive force against the motion of the limb. This allows for the buildup of muscle strength that, in turn, leads to increase use of the limb. Resistive motions such as these can be applied to any body part.

Terms

- End Feel – Occurs when the practitioner moves a client's joint through the range of motion and just before the end point, the practitioner feels a change in the quality of the movement. This sense of resistance, whether based on physiologic or anatomic reasons, is known as the end feel.
- Hard End Feel – Is the feeling of bone rubbing against bone. A common point where this occurs is in the elbow joint.
- Soft End Feel – The limitation that occurs when moving a joint due to the location of soft tissue. Thereby preventing additional movement.
- Empty End Feel – The presence of pain when moving a joint that ends up causing restrictions on the full range of motion.

Hydrotherapy

Hydrotherapy is the practice of using water in the form of liquid, gas, or solid as part of the treatment plan under massage therapy. Heat therapy takes the form of dry heat, moist heat or diathermy. Dry heat consists of heating pads, infrared radiation, or a sauna. Moist heat can come from an immersion bath, spray, heat packs, or a steam bath. Diathermy can be either shortwave or microwave electromagnetic fields onto the tissue. The purpose behind heat therapy is to cause vessels to dilate and increase circulation. Care must be taken to closely monitor the client's body temperature. Cold therapy is also known as cryotherapy. This technique is performed to help reduce the edema, swelling, and painful areas that can occur with an injury. Cold treatments should be applied in short segments of time due to the possibility of tissue injury from the cold. Applying cold to tissues can be in the form of an immersion bath, ice pack, ice massage, through use of a mechanical compressor or through a vasocoolant spray.

Cold Water versus Hot Water

When used as a method of therapy, water can be used in any of the three forms: either as a solid, liquid, or gaseous vapor. As cold water is used for hydrotherapy, it produces an immediate effect of cooling the skin and drawing blood away from the surface of the body. The nerves experience a reduction in their sensitivity levels and the activity of the body's cells in that particular area begin to slow down. After these initial reactions take place, a secondary reaction occurs which causes the skin to become warmer and relaxed. The blood cells on the surface of the skin begin to expand again and nerve impulses increase. The cells nearby increase their activity. When heat therapy is conducted, reactions take place that cause the blood cells from the interior of the body to come up to the surface, producing a reddish area on the skin. These blood vessels dilate and cause an increase in circulation. Body temperature rises and sweating may occur. All of these changes serve to relax the blood vessels and nerves.

Aromatherapy

Aromatherapy is the use of essential oils from natural herbs, flowers, and spices to enhance the massage experience through the sense of smell. These aromas can bring about a specific reaction and are commonly chosen to augment the massage session. Some of the most popular essential oils are chamomile, eucalyptus, jasmine, lavender, and lemongrass. The reactions these oils produce can range from calming, stimulating, refreshing, or relaxing. It is advised not to use these essential oils at their full strength, but instead to combine them with another medium such as carrier oil. This oil serves as a lubricant and helps to blend the oil so it is not as overly concentration, causing irritation to the client. Aromatherapy use can also be applied to scented candles and lotions for use on the client. Prior to the massage, the therapist should consult the intake form or ask the client verbally regarding any allergies or sensitivities to the oils or aromas to be used during the massage.

Body wraps

Body wraps are used for different purposes from relaxation, detoxification, cleansing, and softening the skin. Various types of substances can be used in the wraps from seaweed, volcanic clay and mud. Heat is a common element in wraps whether it comes from an outside source or is obtained from the body. Contraindications for wraps would be the presence of high blood pressure, heart disease, or pregnancy. Body wraps are beneficial in that they provide comfort, security, and warmth, and allow the nutrients to be absorbed in a closed environment rather than dispersed through the air. To perform the wrap, the practitioner must be aware of limitations the client may have on being fully wrapped as well as taking precautions when determining the temperature level of the wraps. The table is laid out with a blanket, a thermal blanket, a towel, and finally a plastic wrap. The client lies down on this plastic and an exfoliation is performed on the client's skin prior to the application of the seaweed or mud. As the seaweed or mud is brushed over the body, the practitioner wraps that portion of the body to prevent heat from escaping. Upon completion of the body, the client is completely engulfed in wraps and is allowed to relax for some time before being assisted through the clean up process by the therapist.

Exfoliation procedure

An exfoliation procedure can be performed in a massage therapy room in which the body is moistened with a sponge rather than made wet in a shower or bath. After the body has been moistened, the practitioner puts salts or exfoliates into his hands and applies them in a circular fashion over the body. Only one surface is exfoliated at a time. A wet towel is used to wipe off the salts, and then a wet loofah is used in the application of soap to the body. After this area has been cleaned, another hot wet cloth is used to remove all residue of soap. The body is then dried off with another towel and the practitioner applies moisturizer all over the body. Exfoliation with salts from the Dead Sea is similar in nature except the salts are mixed with water to form a paste prior to applying to the body.

Therapeutic massage

Therapeutic massage is defined as the process of applying techniques such as effleurage, petrissage, stretching, stroking, etc. on the muscular structure of the body to ease pains in the tendons, ligaments, muscles, and the surface of the skin. This type of massage is intended to create a sense of calmness and relaxation as well as alleviate any pain, stiffness, or soreness in the body. Increased circulation, greater flexibility, improved muscle tone, and improved posture are additional effects that therapeutic massage produces on the body. Having a basic understanding of the human anatomy allows the massage therapist the opportunity to focus on the parts of the body which require additional consideration while enabling him to avoid measures which can cause pain to the client. Physiological changes include lowering of the client's blood pressure, reduction in the heart rate, and slower, deeper breathing, all contribute to the relaxed state of the client.

The massage therapist should pay close attention to areas of concern in the patient's body before, during, and after the massage. Techniques used in the massage have the ability to alleviate any suffering caused by pain or stress. Of particular note is how to relieve the pain from a pain-spasm-pain cycle that is indicated by ischemia (decreased blood flow to the area within a muscle). A proper therapeutic massage increases blood flow to an area and thus creates pleasurable sensations whereas before there was only marked pain. The nerve endings carry these signals to the brain causing the overall feeling of calmness and relaxation throughout the body. To combat ischemia, the massage therapist should focus on breaking the pain-spasm-pain cycle and increase the mobility to that area. Through therapeutic palpations, the exact area of pain can be identified and the therapist can then direct the massage in the area and reduce the amount of lactic acid within the muscle and introduce oxygen and other nutrients to help speed healing.

ATHLETIC MASSAGE

Athletic massage is used to help treat injuries of an athlete thereby increasing the level of strength training, conditioning, and activity. Knowledge of anatomy, physiology, kinesiology, and biomechanics is demanded of the sports massage therapist to assist the athlete and enable him to return to the level of conditioning demanded of his sport. Biomechanics refers to the movement of the body. Soft tissue injuries commonly account for a large portion of the injuries seen by the sports massage therapist. Sports massage therapists must have knowledge of the various muscle groups and how they are used within the sport. It is also important for him to understand the functions of the circulatory system and the nervous system as they all interact with the muscles.

BENEFICIAL EFFECTS

The main effects to an athletic massage are:

- Making oxygen more readily available to allow for repair of the injured body part.
- Waste materials are flushed out through the increased circulation causing increased energy levels.
- The muscles, ligaments, and tendons are stretched allowing for greater flexibility.
- Occurrence of muscle spasms is reduced.
- Adhesions are broken down within the muscle resulting in less scar tissue forming after an injury.
- Collagen fibers come into alignment leading to a stronger healed area.
- Reduces the likelihood of future injuries.
- Acids are released from the body which causes the muscles to "bounce" back after an intense workout.
- Potentially extends the career of an athlete due to fewer injuries.

APPLICATIONS

An athletic massage is broken down into four parts: pre-event massage, post-event massage, restorative or training massage, and rehabilitation massage. Pre-event massage is used before a competition to prepare and invigorate the athlete for the rigors of a competition. It is usually given between 15 minutes to 4 hours before a competition to aid in flexibility and increase circulation. A post-event massage helps to cool the body down and restores the tissues to their normal state. This also helps to relax the athlete through kneading, compression, and light stretching. A restorative massage is used during training and includes deep cross-fiber friction and joint stretches. Rehabilitation massage is used to help heal and repair the muscle tissue after an injury. This type of massage shortens the recuperative time and also minimizes any scar tissue from forming. It helps to build a stronger muscle or joint and allows the athlete to return to training with less likelihood of re-injury.

Rehabilitation Situation

When performing a warm up massage for an athlete, it is important to note any potential problems that could lead to a more serious debilitating injury. If an injury does occur, massage can help to alleviate common problems of the injury. Massage is an effective means to reduce edema and swelling of the affected joint or area. The time that the body needs to recover from the injury is minimized. The scar tissue that is formed at the site of the injury is more flexible and results in less stiffness of the tissue. The athlete can exhibit an increased range of motion of the affected limb as a result of the continued massage. The athlete stands a greater chance of returning to full form in a faster manner than if massage was not considered as part of the rehabilitation program.

CAM Therapy

CAM therapy refers to complementary and alternative medicine that encompasses a more holistic approach to treatment versus allopathic medicine, which relies on medications and surgery for treatment. The types of CAM therapies include the following:

- Acupuncture
- Aromatherapy
- Biofeedback
- Chinese herbal medications
- Chiropractic
- Homeopathy
- Hydrotherapy
- Light therapy
- Massage therapy
- Meditation
- Music therapy
- Prayer and spiritual healing
- Sound therapy
- Yoga

Prenatal Massage

While pregnancy is generally considered a happy moment in a woman's life, it can bring about the onset of many physical changes that cause additional strain and stress upon the body. The physical changes include a shifting of the joints to accommodate the weight gain and stretching of the ligaments to prepare the body for delivery. Some of these changes are due to hormonal reasons and they can cause a pregnant woman to feel additional strain that can only be relieved through rest and relaxation. The most common areas subjected to stresses include the neck, back, hips, legs, and feet. During massage, supporting cushions and bolsters can increase the comfort level of the mother and allow her to fully enjoy the benefits of massage. These benefits include inducing a relaxed state, improvement to the body's circulation, and soothing of the nerves. The most common positions for the mother during massage include lying in the side-lying position and also during the earliest parts of the pregnancy, to lie in the prone position.

Contraindications

It is advised that massage therapy be performed in the prone position only during the first trimester before the new mother is "showing". Reducing the time spent in this position helps to keep the fetus safe. At no time should prenatal massage be performed on the abdominal area. If the mother indicates problems with nausea, vomiting, diarrhea, or unusual vaginal discharge, then massage should be withheld until the physician has been notified. In addition, high blood pressure, lack of fetal movement, severe edema or any abdominal pain experienced by the mother should be immediately referred to the physician as these symptoms can indicate a severe condition such as toxemia or pre-eclampsia. A less serious condition to be aware of in prenatal massage would be the presence of varicose veins. Light effleurage may be performed in these areas, but moderate to heavy massage techniques should be avoided.

Lymph Massage

Lymph massage is closely related to Swedish massage. It is designed to assist with the movement of the lymphatic fluids within the body. When lymph nodes are filled with fluid, a condition known as lymph edema, physicians sometimes recommend lymph drainage massage as a means to alleviate the symptoms. Specific methods used to rhythmically assist with the flow of lymph fluids can cause an increase in metabolism, drain stagnant fluids and toxins, and help to stimulate the immune system. Rhythmic movements in lymph massage also cause a stimulation of the parasympathetic nervous system, which in turn, helps to relieve stress, depression, and combat insomnia. Lymph massage can also help rebalance the chemistry within the body, helps to regenerate tissues, normalizes organs, and also boosts the immune system. Done correctly, the procedure is to gently perform slow movements over the lymph nodes in a circular fashion. Light pressure is then applied in the direction of lymph flow to direct the movement of lymph.

Deep Tissue Massage

Deep tissue massage refers to the massage style that focuses on the deeper muscle and fascia tissues. Various techniques are used in this form of massage to alleviate any tension in the muscular fibers. Massage of this nature can also contribute to psychological and physiological changes in the body. The intent behind this type of massage is to loosen the bonds between the layers of connective tissues. A type of deep tissue massage is known as Rolfing, named after the person who developed this technique, Dr. Ida Rolf. She devised this technique to alleviate tension and structural problems caused by years of one's poor posture and alignment. Rolfing utilizes a heavy- handed technique to realign the body. Performed in a series of many treatments, the massage therapist uses his or her hands, fists, or even knuckles to align the body's movements and create a sense of balance within. A full treatment of Rolfing is a series of 10 treatments although fewer treatments can also lead to improvement. Other deep massage techniques are known as Trager, Hellerwork, and Feldenkrais.

Trigger Point Therapy

Trigger points in the body refer to skeletal muscle areas that are hyperirritable. The presence of palpable nodules in the bands of muscle fibers sometimes causes pain responses that can refer to other parts of the body. Trigger points are classified according to their location in the body and whether or not pain is referred upon palpitation. A common site for trigger points is an acupuncture site, but that does not always hold true as some trigger points are located elsewhere on the body. Activation of a trigger point can be due to causes such as increase in stress levels, an overuse of a particular muscle, and even brought about by an arthritic condition. A brief listing of common trigger points is below:

- active myofascial trigger point
- latent myofascial trigger point
- central trigger point
- attachment trigger point
- primary (or key) trigger point
- satellite trigger point
- associate trigger point

Acupressure

Similar in theory to acupuncture, acupressure is a Chinese technique in which pressure is applied from the hand, elbow, or fingers on acupuncture points across the body. The purpose of acupressure is to bring about relief to the body by balancing the physical and psychological aspects of the body together. Through this method, a person can experience an increased circulatory function, and better pain management. Acupressure is usually performed in combination with diet, exercise, and meditation with the goal of obtaining a holistic lifestyle. Areas of the body where pressure points may be found are along the crown of the head, temple, forehead, and along the upper jaw. Other areas can include the sides and front of the neck, upper arms, elbow joint, and the outside of the thighs and lower legs. Common areas that feel relief through acupressure include the toes, metatarsals, ankles, heels, and Achilles' tendon.

Reflexology

Reflexology is the study by which parts of the body are stimulated in order to produce a reaction in other parts of the body. It is based on the principal that every organ within the body has a corresponding point on either the hands or feet. By applying pressure to the ball of the foot, for example, the practitioner can produce a favorable reaction within the lungs and heart. In addition to the organs, reflexology can also affect glands and muscles. Through use of pressure on the areas corresponding to these glands, tension can be relieved and the body can exhibit an overall increase in function. As an example, the heel of the foot is believed to correspond with the lower back. Pressure on the big toe can lead to relief from headaches. It is important to understand that some skeptics do not believe that this type of massage is beneficial. However, practitioners should not project the opinion that reflexology is a medical cure-all.

Alleviating Stress

When a person undergoes significant stress in his life, it causes physiological and psychological changes in the body. At the physiological level, heart rates can increase, adrenalin rises, sweating may occur, and tightness can be felt within the muscles of the body as the skin prepares for a "fight or flight" response. Psychologically, a person may feel overwhelmed, depressed, moody, sad, and could even turn to outside assistance to deal with the stress, such as alcohol consumption or drug use. Massage is indicated as a means to help alleviate negative stress through the personal human contact inherent in treatment, and through ridding the body of toxins and waste in the cells. During the initial massage therapy consultation, the practitioner should be aware of any indicators of extreme stress and outline a plan that will bring relaxation to the client in a timely manner. At no point should the practitioner assume the role of a psychotherapist or counselor.

Chair Massage

Chair massage can be traced back centuries to its Japanese origins. It is a form of massage that has become increasingly popular and can be found in shopping malls, airports, workplaces, convention center, and other areas where large numbers of people congregate. The style of chair massage allows the client to be fully clothed while seated in a chair in a semi-reclined prone position. Chair massage is an effective way to introduce massage to a person who may exhibit adverse reactions to touch where traditional Swedish massage may be considered too invasive. Chair massage is also used for people who may have been victimized by sexual, physical, or emotional abuse as a way of introducing positive sensations of touch. The application of chair massage enables the practitioner to complete a session in less than 30 minutes, thus making it readily accessible to those on a tight schedule. Finally, chair massage is more cost effective than standard massage sessions, allowing it to be used by people who are less inclined or able to spend money on weekly massages.

Procedure

With the high volume of massages being performed by the practitioner in chair massage, the initial consultation will likely be shorter than in a standard therapeutic setting. The practitioner should still screen for any contraindications to the massage prior to commencement. With the client seated fully clothed and in a prone position, certain techniques such as effleurage and gliding are not possible. Due to the nature of chair massage, friction, percussion and deep touches are the only techniques able to be used in this type of massage. With the client seated in this position, the head, neck, shoulders, back, and hips of the client may be the only areas the practitioner can have access to. In some cases, the client is seated in a supine position to enable the therapist to gain access to the lower legs and feet to perform massage in those areas. Between each client, the practitioner must ensure cleanliness of the chair according to standards. Wiping down the areas that come into contact with the client's skin with an anti-bacterial cleanser is important to control transmission of bacteria or germs. As an alternative, disposable coverings for the face cushion can be used.

Professional Practice

Wellness

The idea of wellness originates from accepting personal responsibility for the state of one's own health. The plan is primarily preventative in that a person sees the potential for disease or ill health and takes the necessary steps to halt that process. The wellness model incorporates three areas: mind, body, and spirit. One's psychological and mental state makes up the area of "mind." A person's physical needs makes up the "body," and one's emotional state and attitude makes up the "spirit." In order to improve one's state of wellness, it is important to adhere to practices that lead to a healthy lifestyle: proper diet, regular exercise, positive mental attitude, balance between work and home, and reducing exposure to potentially stressful situations. When all three areas of the wellness model are addressed, then the person can experience optimum wellness. For the massage therapist, this concept is important as knowledge of the areas that can affect the body is equally as important as those issues and challenges that affect the mind and spirit. Additionally, emotional and mental issues can contribute to pain within the body, again leading the massage therapist to areas needing particular attention during the course of treatment.

Physical strength

A person considering massage therapy should understand that this profession requires a great deal of physical strength. To assist others in massage, the therapist places considerable stress on his own body, which could likely be injured if proper procedures are not followed for administering the massage on a client. Proper stances, exercises for the hands, and good body mechanics will help eliminate some of the stress on the practitioner. It is important to develop good posture, coordination, balance, and stamina to provide the best possible massages for the client with minimal damage to one's self. As the hands are the most important part of the practitioner's tools, flexibility is key to providing control over the speed of the massage, pressure sensitivity, and also ability to conform to the contours of the client's body. Alongside proper physical conditioning, the therapist should also concentrate on his emotional state during the massage and not let outside influences mar the session.

Spa therapists

With a large number of therapists performing in a spa setting, listed below are the types of treatments that the spa therapist may be expected to perform.

- Back treatments
- Parafango
- Bust treatment
- Sauna/Steam bath
- Cellulite treatment
- Scalp treatment
- Exfoliation
- Scotch hose
- Face treatment
- Sea salt treatment
- Foot treatment
- Seaweed wrap
- Herbal wrap
- Swiss shower

- Mud/Clay wrap
- Thalassotherapy
- Mud immersion
- Vichy shower
- Hydrotherapy bath

Insurance Coverage

Massage therapy is useful in assisting with rehabilitation of common injuries such as those sustained in vehicle accidents, repetitive strains, or through athletic injuries. Fibromyalgia, edema, osteoarthritis, and tendonitis are examples of medically diagnosed conditions that may benefit from massage. Along with the diagnosis, a patient can ask for a prescription from the physician to assist with receiving massage therapy to aid with symptoms and help alleviate pain. Although most insurance companies at this time do not approve payment benefits for massage services, it is believed that this policy will change in time as more individuals see the benefit of massage upon these and other conditions. Generally, approval is often given for massage therapy services if the insurance is processed through Worker's Compensation, auto insurance, and through some personal injury cases. Certain states also require insurance companies to reimburse massage therapists for services rendered when a physician has prescribed therapy. A massage therapist should weigh the pros and cons of working with insurance companies. Some considerations may be that only certain procedures are approved and also payment may not be received in a timely manner or may even be denied.

Self-Employed Massage Therapist

One of the first decisions to be made after certification as a massage therapist is whether to go into business for oneself or to work as an employee of a spa, doctor's office, or medical facility. There are pros and cons to each situation. Working as a self-employed massage therapist forces the practitioner to be responsible for his own employment taxes, paying for needed supplies such as office equipment and the massage table, and rental of the facility location. Disadvantages include lack of a formal support team, managing the paperwork for the business side as a self-employed entity, and lack of a steady paycheck due to time needed to building the business. Working in an established environment allows the therapist to have a built in clientele without incurring the overhead costs of doing business. Additionally, the therapist has the support of fellow employees to help with increased client loads. The company would also provide benefits such as vacation, sick leave, and health insurance and be responsible for paying any state and federal employer taxes.

Licensing

Requirements

Licensing requirements vary by state in terms of number of hours of classroom instruction, hands on training, and ongoing continuing education. The purpose of licensing is to ensure that proper training has been completed in order to prevent unethical people from practicing in a manner that would endanger the health and safety of clients. Since the individual states set the guidelines by which a person can be certified as a massage therapist, licenses are not automatically recognized from one city, county, or state to another. It is up to the individual to research with the county commissioner's office, the city attorney, or the county clerk to see if licenses are recognized from other areas. The educational requirements to obtain licensure are training in anatomy, physiology, and pathology, as well as knowledge of the effect that massage has on the body. Additional requirements include knowledge of massage techniques to include any contraindications and precautions to take on behalf of the client. Finally, training on methods to help develop a trusting relationship with one's clientele is important to running a successful business.

Revoking License

The potential exists for a practitioner to have his license revoked if they exhibit any behaviors deemed harmful to their clients or violate ethical standards within the realm of massage therapy. Other forms of punishment could initially include license suspension or cancellation. Reasons for revoking the license could be engaging in deceit in order to obtain the license, being convicted of a felony, or engaging in any form of prostitution under the guise of massage therapy. Additionally, performing duties while under the influence of drugs, alcohol, or otherwise compromising the safety of the client are grounds for suspension or revocation of license. Running one's business practice under a false or assumed name, willfully endangering the welfare and health of the client, and prescribing medications without a physician's license can also lead to cancellation of the license. The health community strives to promote integrity within this field and has struggled for years with a negative connotation associated with it. Thus, adherence to these guidelines is mandatory to maintain their high standards.

Licenses and Permits

- Fictitious name statement (DBA) –Differentiates between owner's name and name of the business. Filed with the county clerk's office; prevents others from securing the exact same business name.
- Business License – Required if operating a business within a city.
- Massage License – Allows the practitioner to receive fees for services.
- Sales Tax Permit –If practitioner sells products or charges tax.
- Planning and Zoning permits –Ensures that business meets zoning requirements (especially if the business is run out of owner's home).
- Building safety permit – After an inspection to determine that a facility is deemed safe for use by both employees and clients, a building permit will be issued in the name of the business.
- Employers Identification Number (EIN) – Number assigned to the business for federal tax purposes. This only applied to partnerships and businesses that hire employees.
- Provider's number – An ID number to help identify a specific practitioner for the purposes of insurance paperwork and claims information.

Registering

A massage therapist has the option of registering their business as either a sole proprietor, partnership, LLC, or a corporation.

- Sole proprietor: owner assumes all responsibility for the business whether it is from a financial or obligatory standpoint; individual is legally responsible for all failures of the business, may be held accountable in the event of lawsuits or debt. Advantage: owner is not accountable to a board or group of shareholders.
- Partnership: two or more individuals share in the successes and failures of the business with the risk held equally by all. It is similar to a sole proprietorship in that the group of owners can be held personally responsible for all activities of the business.
- Limited liability Corporation (LLC): is a combination of a partnership and a corporation. Some benefits similar to that of a corporation are present, however, the extent of the paperwork involved is not as in depth as that of a corporation. Additionally, an LLC offers more protection of one's personal assets in the event of a lawsuit. Finally, a corporation assigns management of the business to a board of directors who share in the policy and decision-making.

Liability Insurance

Liability insurance covers the business in the event of any injuries on the property, or litigation brought against the business. If the business is run out of the home, some of these incidents may be covered under the homeowner's policy. Professional liability insurance guards against the possibility of litigation brought forth by a client who feels that the practitioner caused injury or harm due to negligence in services received. Automobile insurance covers the passengers and the vehicle in the event of an accident. Coverage ranges from liability only to full coverage regardless of fault. This insurance should be obtained as an individual, but also if a vehicle is used for business purposes and travel. Worker's compensation insurance covers those employees who have been hired to work for the practitioner and who may become injured while on the job. Medical and health insurance can also be provided for the owner/practitioner and all of his employees. Disability insurance covers any employees who become disabled due to injuries sustained on the job.

Expenses

Start up expenses for a massage therapy practice can include the following:

- Work location –Leasing vs. working from home.
- Utilities
- Equipment – This can include portable as well as stationary massage tables and chairs, bolsters, towels and linens, and massage oils and lotions, hydrotherapy tubs
- Furniture – Desk and chairs needed for the waiting area, office, and conference room as well as a personal work desk for the massage therapist.
- Office Supplies – Computer, fax machine, file cabinets, writing utensils, appointment books, etc.
- Advertising and printing expenses – To include the costs of marketing your massage therapy business either in print, TV, or on the radio.

Business Ethics

In order to run a successful and ethical massage therapy practice, the massage therapist should adhere to the following guidelines to provide the best possible level of service to his clientele. Presenting oneself professionally both in attitude and in appearance, while projecting a positive demeanor is important to make your client feel at ease. Treating each client with the same level of respect regardless of gender or age also shows concern for the client as does adhering to the schedule in order to provide ample time for each client. Additionally, being able to run one's business in an organized manner shows good business skills and allows attentiveness to one's clients. Joining a professional organization shows the practitioner ways to increase his skills in the field and also provides an opportunity for networking and professional growth. Finally, to perform in an ethical manner, the massage therapist should obey all the laws and legal requirements while doing business and also keep one's personal life separate from the business affairs.

Marketing Plan

Marketing is the process used to promote one's business with the intent to increase income and build up the client base. Several types of marketing strategies include advertising and promotions in the form of written brochures, print ads in newspapers, websites and other publications, media outlets such as radio and television, and also through referrals from repeat customers. A successful marketing plan focuses on the needs of the client and addresses how one's business can meet those needs. Marketing should be an on-going process with the intent being to make changes as some strategies bring about more clientele versus others. The types of marketing conducted are influenced by the budget, time constraints, and also the time involved in implementing them. A marketing plan is the outline by which a business determines the actions necessary to achieve a certain goal. Most marketing plans are created to span a period of one year up to five years.

Staffing

As the massage therapy practice grows, it may become necessary to add to one's staff to increase the capabilities of serving more clients. Some businesses hire massage therapists as an independent contractor or as a full time employee. As an independent contractor, the practitioner is responsible for paying his own taxes and will need to file tax forms 1099 and 1096 if he exceeds $600.00 in income during the previous year. As a full time employee, the employer is responsible for providing an hourly paycheck and a benefit package. In either case, the person hired has the ability to help the business succeed or fail based on his professionalism and how personable he or she is with the clients. When seeking out new employees, it is important to verify all credentials and licensing, ensure that appropriate training is provided, and work with the person to help him achieve the business goals.

Boundaries

Boundaries are defined as the personal comfort zones that each person maintains for his own security. Boundaries are intangible and unseen. The acceptable distance from the person's body to another individual varies and is dependent upon the first person's past experiences in life that determines what he or she feels is acceptable. Boundaries can be divided into four types: physical, emotional, intellectual, or sexual. They serve as a personal protective device and during the course of the massage, the practitioner should be aware of any subtle nuances that would let him know that the client may be at the verge of discomfort. It is important that the practitioner be aware of the client's boundary levels and exhibits the utmost in respect, concern, and professionalism.

Professional Boundaries

- Location of services received –Location in which massage services are received. Consider the client's safety, comfort, and security.
- Interpersonal space –Distance between practitioner and client; and is commonly one of the most crossed boundaries in some individuals.
- Appearance –Especially good hygiene and modest clothing.
- Self-disclosure – Any personal information given from the client to the practitioner should be directly related to the treatment and therapy at hand.
- Language- The choice of words, tone, phrasing, and intonation do much to convey a safe, secure, peaceful environment.
- Touch – Touch during a massage is necessary, however, only that part of the body that is being massaged should be in skin-to-skin contact. The genital area is to be avoided and draping should be provided for all areas not being massaged.
- Time – Adherence to the set appointment times shows respect for the client's time and other personal activities. Also, open communication regarding policies for missed appointments, no shows, and lateness helps to define the boundaries between the client and the practitioner.
- Money – Defining the fee schedule for services rendered in advance of the therapeutic sessions helps to define the boundaries.

Transference

Transference occurs when a client personalizes the relationship between himself and the practitioner and then projects feelings towards that person. These feelings can manifest as either positive or negative as the client projects characteristics of a person from a former relationship onto the therapist. It is shown through behaviors such as attempting to initiate conversations unrelated to the therapy session, through giving of gifts to the practitioner or therapist, through proposing friendship or a relationship outside of the therapy environment, or by becoming angry, depressed or sad when advances are rejected. Counter transference works in the opposite manner: the therapist or practitioner interjects feelings towards a client. Examples can include excitability over the client's appointment time or thinking about the client at times outside of the therapy session. They also can manifest as dread over a client's appointment time or by feeling anger if the therapist believes that the client is not responding to treatment methods. It is important to address these concerns by acknowledging them and finding an alternative practitioner to resume treatment or simply discontinue treating that client at one's facility.

Pharmacology

Pharmacology is the study of the effects that drugs have on living organisms. With a large number of individuals on prescription therapy, it may be common for the massage practitioner to encounter someone who is on drug therapy, yet may need the services of a massage therapist. Medications can cause side effects that, if not made known to the massage practitioner, will continue in spite of treatment. As an example, some medications cause muscle pains and weakness. With the knowledge of the types of medications a client is taking, the therapist can then adapt the massage sessions to reflect avoidance of those areas in question. Also, some medications may provide the same benefits as those obtained by massage. In these cases, the individual may see a decreased need for the medication in light of the relief seen through massage. Part of the initial consultation can include a list of the medications, supplements, vitamins, and herbs the client may be taking.

Drugs

Drugs are any chemical or herbal substances that are used in relieving symptoms of an illness or disease. The term "drug" can also be used to refer to those illegal substances, which alters the mind's perception and the body's movements. Oftentimes, the drugs prescribed by a physician can produce adverse side effects on the human body that can interfere with any benefits obtained from use of the drug. Some drugs have the ability to affect an entire system of the body, such as drugs affecting the circulatory system, or the drugs can cause only a localized reaction, such as alleviating the pain of a broken leg. Drugs do not affect all individuals in the same manner as a person's age, body weight, and height help to determine how fast the body absorbs the drug. Drugs are given a generic name upon creation by a pharmaceutical company. A specific trade name is then given to help consumers identify it and make it easier to remember. Drugs are classified according to their therapeutic abilities, thus, the same drug can be found in more than one classification by use.

Categories

Medications are taken to assist healing from certain ailments. The following is a list of the various drug categories.

- Drugs treating skin conditions such as allergic reactions and fungal infections
- Musculoskeletal and anti-inflammatory drugs
- Gastrointestinal medications
- Respiratory medications and antihistamines
- Cardiovascular medications
- Urinary system medications
- Drugs treating tumors or cancers
- Drugs treating the endocrine system such as those for diabetes or for hormone replacement
- Drugs treating the reproductive system

- Anti-infective drugs including antibiotics and those drugs that combat bacterial infections
- Analgesics, sedatives, and hypnotic drugs to help relieve pain, calm a person's nerves and aid in insomnia
- Psychotropic drugs for treating alcoholism and drug abuse
- Anti-convulsion drugs

HERBAL SUPPLEMENTS

Herbal remedies have been around for many years and their basis can be found in many cultural groups such as the Native Americans or Chinese. Herbs have many uses from cooking to decoration and to healing. Depending on the purpose and need for the plant, all parts may be used from the flowers and seeds down to the roots. Herbs, rather than chemically based drugs, are more commonly prescribed by physicians in other parts of the world. Approximately 25% of prescription drugs come from a natural botanical source rather than being strictly, chemically manufactured in a lab environment. People tend to purchase herbs and supplements as a means of preventing diseases, maintain good health, and as an additional form of treatment in conjunction with standard pharmaceutical treatment methods. The massage therapist should have an understanding of the effects of herbal supplements because of their widespread use and also because the relief they provide could interact with prescription medications.

Texas Massage Therapy Practice Test

Want to take this practice test in an online interactive format?
Check out the online resources page, which includes interactive practice questions and much more: **mometrix.com/resources719/texmassthwrex**

1. Which of the following accounts for approximately 16% of the human body?

a. Integumentary system.
b. Skeletal system.
c. Circulatory system.
d. Respiratory system.

2. Which of the following systems is comprised of 206 individual organs?

a. Integumentary system.
b. Skeletal system.
c. Circulatory system.
d. Respiratory system.

3. Which of the following is comprised of smooth, voluntary, and cardiac tissues?

a. Integumentary system.
b. Skeletal system.
c. Circulatory system.
d. Muscular system.

4. What three main organs make up the nervous system?

a. Brain, spinal cord, and ATP.
b. Brain, skin, and nerves.
c. Brain, spinal cord, and nerves.
d. ATP, spinal cord, and nerves.

5. Which of the following systems acts like the nervous system, but with slower reaction time and longer-lasting effects?

a. Integumentary system.
b. Skeletal system.
c. Cardiovascular system.
d. Endocrine system.

6. Which of the following systems is a closed circuit whose main function is transportation through a network of vessels?

a. Lymphatic system.
b. Skeletal system.
c. Cardiovascular system.
d. Endocrine system.

7. Which of the following systems transports a whitish, watery fluid called lymph?

a. Lymphatic system.
b. Urinary system.
c. Cardiovascular system.
d. Endocrine system.

8. Which of the following systems produces waste in the kidney that moves to the ureters, and is stored in the urinary bladder?

a. Lymphatic system.
b. Urinary system.
c. Respiratory system.
d. Digestive system.

9. Which of the following systems functions as a means to rid the body of carbon dioxide?

a. Lymphatic system.
b. Urinary system.
c. Respiratory system.
d. Digestive system.

10. Which of the following systems include both the teeth and the pharynx?

a. Lymphatic system.
b. Urinary system.
c. Respiratory system.
d. Digestive system.

11. In the male reproductive system, what two organs make up the genitalia?

a. The gonads and the penis.
b. The penis and the scrotum.
c. The prostate and the vas deferens.
d. The scrotum and the gonads.

12. What organ is considered the female gonads?

a. Ovaries
b. Fallopian tube.
c. Vagina
d. Uterine.

13. Which of the following refer to the division of the cranial and sacral segments of the spinal cord?

a. Craniosacral division.
b. Sacralcranium division.
c. Cranio and sacral aspects.
d. Proprioception.

14. Which of the following types of membrane is found in closed cavities in the body?

a. Cutaneous membranes.
b. Serous membranes.
c. Mucous membranes.
d. Connective tissue membranes.

15. What information can the width of the epiphyseal plate tell a doctor?

a. The strength of a bone.
b. The estimated adult height of an individual.
c. The probability of osteoporosis.
d. The number of breaks a bone has had.

16. What is the purpose of the synergist in movement?

a. Add support to the contracting prime mover.
b. Counteract the prime mover.
c. Relax as the antagonists contracts.
d. Act as the main muscle in the movement.

17. Neurons are named for the direction they move. What are the three types neurons found in the body?

a. Motor, Schwann, Interneurons.
b. Sensory, Cranial, Interneurons.
c. Sensory, Involuntary, Interneurons.
d. Sensory, Motor, Interneurons.

18. What is the main mechanism behind the functioning of nonsteroid hormones?

a. Negative feedback.
b. Hypersecretion.
c. Second messenger mechanism.
d. Positive feedback.

19. What is the difference between the tunica externa in an artery compared to that in a vein?

a. The tunica externa is thinner in arteries than in veins.
b. The tunica externa is thicker in arteries than in veins.
c. Arteries do not have a tunica externa.
d. Veins do not have a tunica externa.

20. What percentage of the body moves lymph in to the thoracic duct?

a. 100%.
b. 75%.
c. 50%.
d. 25%.

21. What is the main function of the respiratory membrane?

a. To line the respiratory tract with a layer of mucus.
b. To act to separate air into the alveoli or the blood in the capillaries.
c. To serve as a barrier to the outside air.
d. To allow consistent oxygen flow into the blood stream.

22. Which of the following structures begins the process of digestion?

a. Stomach.
b. Small intestine.
c. Teeth.
d. Esophagus.

23. What is manipulated in the craniosacral system during a craniosacral therapeutic session?

a. Dura mater.
b. Interstitial fluid.
c. Pia mater.
d. Cerebrospinal fluid.

24. What occurs during the process of resorption?

a. Fluid moves from the renal tubules into the blood stream.
b. Fluid moves from the blood stream into the renal tubules.
c. Fluid is filtered more than once.
d. Elimination cannot occur and fluid is processed through the body again.

25. What is the term that refers to a body standing erect with hands at the sides and palms facing forward?

a. Anatomical Position (western medicine).
b. Anatomical Position (oriental medicine).
c. Prone.
d. Supine.

26. The plane that goes from top to bottom, which divides the body in left and right sides directly in the middle is referred to as which of the following?

a. Sagittal.
b. Frontal.
c. Transverse.
d. Midsagittal.

27. Which of the following are located in the dorsal cavity?

a. The abdominopelvic cavity.
b. The lungs.
c. The thoracic cavity.
d. None of the above.

28. Which of the following is not a major muscle of the head?

a. Orbicularis oculi.
b. Zygomaticus.
c. Semimembranosus.
d. Masseter.

29. Which muscle has an origin at the external occipital protuberance ligamentum nuchae and an insertion at the lateral third of clavicle acromion?

a. Teres major.
b. Latissimus dorsi.
c. Trapezius.
d. Teres minor.

30. Which of the following muscles has an action of medial rotation and adduction of the humerus?

a. Supraspinatus.
b. Latissimus dorsi.
c. Trapezius.
d. Teres minor.

31. Which of the following is a depressor of the scapula?

a. Upper trapezius.
b. Pectoralis minor.
c. Lower trapezius.
d. Serratus anterior.

32. What is occurring when a muscle contracts but no movement is produced?

a. Twitch contraction.
b. Tetanic contraction.
c. Isotonic contraction.
d. Isometric contraction.

33. What is occurring when a muscle experiences an involuntary quick movement?

a. Twitch contraction.
b. Tetanic contraction.
c. Isotonic contraction.
d. Isometric contraction.

34. What is the attachment which is on the more stationary bone?

a. Tendon.
b. Origin.
c. Insertion.
d. Bursae.

35. Which of the following connective tissues serve to anchor muscle to bone?

a. Bursae.
b. Tendon.
c. Ligament.
d. Sarcomere.

36. The iliopsoas and the adductor muscles work to move what part of the body?

a. Head and neck.
b. Arms.
c. Thigh.
d. Feet and ankles.

37. What function does the orbicularis oculi serve?

a. Bring lips together.
b. Elevates corners of lips.
c. Close eyes.
d. Opens eyes.

38. Which of the following joints are located in the skull?

a. Synarthroses.
b. Amphiarthroses.
c. Diarthroses.
d. There are no joints in the skull.

39. What is the most common type of join found in the human body?

a. Synarthroses.
b. Amphiarthroses.
c. Diarthroses.
d. Double joints.

40. A ball and socket joint can be found in what region of the body?

a. Shoulder.
b. Fingers.
c. Spine.
d. Knee.

41. Which of the following would a neurologist use to determine the specific point of damage on the spine?

a. Spinal fracture test.
b. Dermatomes.
c. Motor reflex test.
d. Meridians.

42. How many primary meridians make up the human body?

a. 10
b. 11.
c. 12.
d. 13.

43. Exposure to extreme heat, surgery, and illnesses are all examples of what on the body?

a. Homeostasis.
b. Disease.
c. Stress.
d. Heterostasis.

44. Which of the following typically results from a hypersecretion of glucocorticoids?

a. Addison's disease.
b. Cushing syndrome.
c. Type I diabetes.
d. Virilizing tumor.

45. Which of the following techniques would be used by an individual participating preparing to run in a marathon in 3 days?

a. Carbohydrate loading.
b. Protein loading.
c. Glycogenesis.
d. Antioxidant treatments.

46. What is required for muscles to contract?

a. Myofilaments.
b. Z-lines.
c. ATP molecules.
d. Actin.

47. What type of muscle contraction is occurring is a person is sitting up straight?

a. Isotonic contraction.
b. Tetanic contraction.
c. Tonic contraction.
d. Isometric contraction.

48. What type of movement is occurring in the angle between the forearm and humorous decreases?

a. Flexion.
b. Extension.
c. Abduction.
d. Adduction.

49. Moving your arms straight out to the sides requires what type of movement?

a. Flexion.
b. Extension.
c. Abduction.
d. Adduction

50. The downward motion of tapping your foot requires what type of movement?

a. Rotation.
b. Supination.
c. Dorsiflexion.
d. Plantar flexion.

51. Shaking your head "No" requires what type of movement?

a. Rotation.
b. Supination.
c. Abduction.
d. Adduction.

52. What must be stimulated in order to determine movement of the body?

a. Muscles.
b. Chakras.
c. Proprioceptors.
d. Bones.

53. Receptors that have some type of covering over their endings can be referred to as what?

a. Closed-end receptors.
b. Encapsulated.
c. Unencapsulated.
d. Sheathed bulb receptors.

54. In an individual with anorexia, what will the body rely on for energy once the fat stores are used up?

a. Calcium.
b. Carbohydrates.
c. Proteins.
d. Simple sugars.

55. What can occur from a deficiency of vitamin C?

a. Scurvy.
b. Night blindness.
c. Nerve problems.
d. Pernicious anemia.

56. Which of the following minerals, when deficient leads to fatigue and anemia?

a. Calcium.
b. Cobalt.
c. Iodine.
d. Copper.

57. If an individual has a deficiency in calories and protein, what disorder are they likely to have?

a. Anorexia nervosa.
b. Protein deficiency.
c. Pro-caloric malnutrition.
d. Protein-calorie malnutrition.

58. If a patient complains of pain in the left lumbar region, what organ is probably affected?

a. Descending colon.
b. Stomach.
c. Liver.
d. Kidneys.

59. Which function is responsible for maintaining equilibrium in the body?

a. Homeostasis.
b. Feedback loop.
c. Biorhythm.
d. Brain functions.

60. Which of the following has a phospholipid bilayer with proteins as its structure?

a. Ribosomes.
b. Mitochondria.
c. Plasma membrane.
d. Lysosomes.

61. If you get a paper cut on your finger, what type of tissue have you damaged?

a. Epithelial tissue.
b. Connective tissue.
c. Muscle tissues.
d. Nervous tissue.

62. Dr. Wright determined that 2-year-old Sammy will grow to be about 6-feet tall. What part of the bone did Dr. Wright look at to determine this number?

a. Diaphysis.
b. Articular cartilage.
c. Epiphyseal plate.
d. Endosteum.

63. When faced with a stressful situation, John's body began sweating. Why did this occur?

a. Activation of the parasympathetic system.
b. Activation of the sympathetic system.
c. Activation of the endocrine system.
d. Activation of the nervous system.

64. The ripple look of a toned stomach is the result of what type of muscle pattern?

a. Multipennate.
b. Fusiform.
c. Strap.
d. Tricipital.

Use the following to answer question 65:

A new client comes in for a massage. She is a 35-year-old school teacher recommended by her doctor for massage. She is complaining about back and shoulder problems and states that she had shoulder surgery 8 months ago. As you read through the intake form, you also see that she is two months pregnant, has had massage in the past, and has migraine headaches. She also tells you that yesterday she fell while running and may have sprained her ankle but has not gone to the doctor.

65. Which of this client's medical situation is contraindicated for massage?

a. Pregnancy.
b. Shoulder surgery 8 months ago.
c. Migraine headaches.
d. Possible sprain.

66. If a massage therapist is calling a doctor to talk about a client with widespread pain, how would she describe this to the doctor?

a. Pain all over.
b. Fibromyalgia.
c. Hypersensitivity.
d. Hypo-muscle sensitivity.

67. Which of the following is probably not a part of the etiology of polycystic kidney disease?

a. Cysts on the kidneys.
b. Inherited.
c. Mutation on PKD1 gene.
d. 5% have end-stage renal disease.

Use the following to answer questions 68-69:

A scientist studies the pattern of diseases and finds that a disease has spread from one country to the next on a large scale. Seeing that individuals with the disease experience chest pain, coughing blood, fever, chills, and weight loss, the scientist determines it is tuberculosis. Additionally, he notices that there are a large number of individuals who had silicosis prior to contracting tuberculosis. As the scientist discusses this situation with other doctors, they decide all healthcare workers must wear masks while near and treating these patients.

68. Why must healthcare workers wear masks when caring for these patients?

a. It is an airborne illness.
b. These patients emit a foul order.
c. They are susceptible to other germs the healthcare workers may have.
d. The air quality in the country may be very poor.

69. What would a healthcare worker refer to coughing blood, fever, chills, and weight loss as?

a. Symptoms.
b. Signs.
c. Complaints.
d. Idiopathic indications.

70. Which mood-altering chemicals are released during massage that could have a profound effect on an individual with depression?

a. Serotonin.
b. Estrogen.
c. Adrenalin.
d. Oxytocin.

71. Which of the following would be most appropriate for an individual with autism?

a. No massage.
b. Light, gentle strokes.
c. Firm, purposeful touch.
d. Hands and feet only.

72. How does a general relaxation massage benefit an individual with anxiety?

a. Influences the automatic nervous system.
b. Stimulates.
c. Reduces hormones, causing anxiety.
d. Anxiety is contraindicated.

73. What must a therapist be careful of in an individual with osteoporosis?

a. Breaking a bone.
b. Tearing a tendon.
c. Causing emotional distress.
d. Spreading the disease.

74. Which of the following refers to a signed document that gives the therapist permission to work on an individual?

a. Right of refusal.
b. Informed consent.
c. Contract.
d. Intake questionnaire.

Use the following to answer questions 75-76:

You meet a new client and provide them with all the required paperwork, including an intake questionnaire and informed consent. After they have completed and signed the paper work, you review it and ask a few questions. You find out the individual has been under a lot of stress and emotional turmoil due to the recent loss of a spouse. They tell you a friend recommends massage as a way to relax. You can understand how they are feeling because you too recently lost a loved one. After the initial interview, you begin the massage. Your client asks for a gentle massage and lets you know they are not comfortable with massage on the face and gluts.

75. What would be occurring if your client began developing feelings for you beyond the client-therapist relationship and they state you are a lot like their deceased spouse?

a. Violating legal boundaries.
b. Violating personal boundaries.
c. Transference.
d. Countertransference.

76. What would be occurring if you developed feelings for your client beyond the client-therapist relationship?

a. Violating legal boundaries.
b. Violating personal boundaries.
c. Transference.
d. Countertransference.

77. How could you as a massage therapist cross your client's personal boundaries?

a. Listen to your client throughout the massage.
b. Massage their face.
c. Listen and offer your assessment or opinion of their situation.
d. Give them the name of a grief-counseling group.

78. How could you as a massage therapist cross legal or ethical boundaries?

a. Listen to your client throughout the massage.
b. Massage their face.
c. Listen and offer your assessment or opinion of their situation.
d. Give them the name of a grief-counseling group.

79. What is one way in which different types of healthcare workers, for example, a massage therapist and a physician, can communicate?

a. Medical terminology.
b. At conferences.
c. Using notes to the client.
d. Like normal people.

80. A massage therapist that rents a room from a spa would probably file their taxes under which category?

a. Employee.
b. Corporation.
c. Independent contractor.
d. Dependant.

81. How does a massage therapist maintain an individual's privacy throughout the massage?

a. Keeping the door shut.
b. Draping.
c. Turning the lights on low.
d. Massaging with your eyes closed.

82. Why would a therapist typically not massage the armpit?

a. Endangerment site.
b. The client is ticklish.
c. The client does not shave.
d. The client has body odor.

83. Suppose a client comes for a massage and states that his back pain began about 1 year ago, in terms of level of the condition, what would this back pain be considered?

a. Acute.
b. A sign.
c. Chronic.
d. A symptom.

84. What should you do if a client comes in for a massage and is ill?

a. Send them home.
b. Perform light massage.
c. Refer them to a physician.
d. Wear gloves.

85. A massage therapist talks about their client's illnesses and conditions, using names, at the dinner table each night. What has been violated?

a. Confidentiality.
b. Personal boundaries.
c. Trust.
d. Nothing.

86. Which of the following would help a therapist document their work on a client?

a. HIPAA.
b. S.O.A.P.
c. ICD-10-CM.
d. HPI.

87. Which of the following would contraindicate lymphatic massage?

a. Congenital defect.
b. Benign neoplasm.
c. Malignant neoplasm.
d. Chronic pain.

88. A sprain with 10% fiber tear would be classified as what type of sprain?

a. Grade One.
b. Grade Two.
c. Grade Three.
d. Grade Four.

89. A traumatic injury that results in 60% muscle fiber tear and swelling would be considered which of the following?

a. First-degree strain.
b. Second-degree strain.
c. Third-degree strain.
d. Fourth-degree strain.

90. Which type of bone fracture results in the bone being completely separated?

a. Incomplete.
b. Complete.
c. Open.
d. Fracture dislocation.

91. On which of the following types of headache would you consider performing trigger point therapy?

a. Migraine.
b. Cluster.
c. Tension.
d. Cervicogenic.

92. An individual would be experiencing which of the following if they were in shock due to loss of blood?

a. Cardiogenic shock.
b. Hypovolemic shock.
c. Neurogenic shock.
d. Anaphylactic shock.

93. Which of the following is not considered an upper respiratory infection?

a. Rhinitis.
b. Pharyngitis.
c. Laryngitis.
d. Bronchitis.

94. If an individual states that they have hypernatremia, what is happening in their body?

a. Potassium imbalance.
b. Sodium imbalance.
c. Calcium imbalance.
d. Dehydration.

95. Which of the following is not a purpose of massage?

a. To increase cell metabolism.
b. To heal illness.
c. To increase ROI.
d. To relieve pain.

96. Breaking up adhesions using petrissage would be considered what type of effect on the body?

a. Mechanical.
b. Physiological.
c. Psychological.
d. Pain-relieving.

97. On what does lymph rely to be moved through the body?

a. Blood flow.
b. Voluntary muscles.
c. Involuntary muscles.
d. Massage.

98. What is one result of over stimulation of the nervous system to muscles?

a. Relaxation.
b. Pain.
c. Spasm.
d. Injury.

99. Which of the following is typically the first stroke to begin a massage?

a. Petrissage.
b. Friction.
c. Effleurage.
d. Tapotement.

100. Which of the following strokes can enhance fluid movement of deeper tissue?

a. Petrissage.
b. Friction.
c. Effleurage.
d. Tapotement.

101. Which of the following best describes abnormal restrictions to joint movements?

a. Reduced range of motion.
b. Reduced joint movement.
c. Passive joint movement.
d. Active joint movement.

102. Which of the following is indicated for massage?

a. Asthma.
b. Abdominal aneurysm.
c. Bursitis.
d. Edema.

103. Which of the following best describes an effect of hydrotherapy that affects the entire body?

a. Local effect.
b. Systemic effect.
c. Reflex effect.
d. Thermal effect.

104. Which of the following refer to the study of movement?

a. Biomechanics.
b. Synergists.
c. Kinesiology.
d. Massage therapy.

105. In Kinesiology, which of the following aspects of an assessment would include passive ROM?

a. History.
b. Observation.
c. Palpation.
d. Specialized testing.

106. Which of the following organelles are found only in the small intestine?

a. Cilia.
b. Flagella.
c. Microvilli.
d. Centrioles.

107. In terms of an active transport system, which of the following move molecules against the concentration gradient?

a. Phagocytosis.
b. Pinocytosis.
c. Permease System.
d. Filtration.

Use the following vignette to answer questions 108-111:

> Newly licensed massage therapist Amy immediately opens an office. She figures she will figure out the business aspect of owning a business as so goes. She has named her massage business "The Healing Touch" and has created signs, advertising materials, and business cards with a logo. She is on time for all massage appointments, keeps the waiting room neat and stocked with information about massage, and has her license displayed on the wall. The only records Amy keeps are the client records and she notes the date and amount paid for all massages from that client. Amy has purchased insurance including Property Damage, Bodily Injury Liability, and Malpractice insurance. Her insurance agent also suggests that she purchase Business and Personal Property Loss and Disability insurance, but Amy declines.

108. If Amy's office undergoes a flood, leading to $1,000 in damage, why will she have to pay out-of-pocket expenses?

a. She did not purchase enough Property Damage insurance.
b. She did not purchase Business & Personal Property Loss insurance.
c. Floods are not covered under any insurance.
d. The damage did not meet her deductible.

109. A client fell in the waiting room of Amy's office, why does Amy feel secure that she is covered in this incident?

a. She has Malpractice insurance.
b. She has Property Damage and Bodily Injury Liability insurance.
c. She rents the office, so the landlord is responsible.
d. The injury did not occur during the massage, so it is the client's responsibility.

110. In the above vignette, what, concerning the business aspect, does Amy neglect to do?

a. Create a professional image.
b. Purchase Disability insurance.
c. Develop a business plan.
d. Advertise in the newspaper.

111. What has Amy created by developing a logo and marketing materials?

a. A business plan.
b. Professional image.
c. Additional bills.
d. A sound marketing plan.

112. A client comes in for a massage and complains that due to a back injury, they currently rely on their family members to take care of their home. To whom might you refer this client in order to increase their quality of life and independence?

a. Chiropractor.
b. Acupuncturist.
c. Occupational Therapist.
d. Physical Therapist.

113. What are the three steps to take for a primary survey when faced with an individual who may not be breathing?

a. Airway, breathing, circulation.
b. Clear the area, check breathing, check for neck injury.
c. Airway, clear the area, circulation.
d. Call 911, clear the area, check Breathing.

114. Which of the following is the most efficient standing position for a massage therapist?

a. Symmetric standing.
b. Asymmetric standing.
c. Knees slightly bent.
d. Knees locked.

115. Which of the following refers to a passive joint movement?

a. Osteokinematic movement.
b. Arthrokinematic movement.
c. Hinge movement.
d. Joint movement.

116. What is the point at which injury would occur to a joint?

a. Physiologic barrier.
b. Pathologic barrier.
c. Anatomic barrier.
d. Range of motion.

117. For which massage therapy setting would it be most beneficial for a therapist to know and understand various dysfunctions of the body?

a. Private practice.
b. Medical office.
c. Spa.
d. Chiropractor's office.

118. On what bodily system does hydrotherapy focus?

a. Integumentary.
b. Muscle.
c. Autonomic nervous.
d. Respiratory.

119. Which of the following massage techniques could leave the client feeling fatigued and listless for up to 48 hours after the massage?

a. Hydrotherapy.
b. Swedish massage.
c. Lymphatic drainage.
d. Reflexology.

120. Which of the following is contraindicated for lymphatic drainage?

a. Simple edema.
b. Low blood pressure.
c. High blood pressure.
d. Traveler's edema.

121. Which of the following techniques would be used for an individual at the end stages of a terminal illness?

a. Palliative care.
b. Deep tissue.
c. Swedish.
d. This is contraindicated.

122. What are the most complex units in the body?

a. Cells.
b. Tissues.
c. Organs.
d. Systems.

123. Approximately what percentage of the human body is composed of oxygen, carbon, hydrogen, and nitrogen?

a. 90%.
b. 93%.
c. 96%.
d. 100%.

124. Which of the following has no nucleus?

a. White blood cells.
b. Sperm cells.
c. Red blood cells.
d. Liver cells.

125. Which of the following describes epithelia tissue that is flat and scalelike?

a. Squamous.
b. Cuboidal.
c. Columnar.
d. Transitional.

126. Which system includes oil glands?

a. Integumentary.
b. Skeletal.
c. Reproductive.
d. Lymphatic.

127. Which of the following risk factors of disease cannot be controlled by the individual?

a. Lifestyle.
b. Genetic.
c. Environment.
d. Stress.

128. Which of the following membranes are only found within closed cavities?

a. Cutaneous.
b. Serous.
c. Mucous.
d. Connective.

129. Which of the following membranes line surfaces that open to the outside of the body?

a. Cutaneous.
b. Serous.
c. Mucous.
d. Connective.

130. What is the unit within each skeletal muscle fiber?

a. Microfilaments.
b. Bursae.
c. Myofilaments.
d. Actin.

131. What are the muscles of the trunk from deep to superior?

a. Internal oblique, Transversus abdominis, Rectus abdominis, External oblique.
b. External oblique, Internal oblique, Transversus abdominis, Rectus abdominis.
c. Rectus abdominis, Internal oblique, Transversus abdominis, External oblique
d. Transversus abdominis, Internal oblique, Rectus abdominis, External oblique.

132. Which of the following is not a part of the adductor group for the lower extremities?

a. Adductor longus.
b. Gracilis.
c. Iliopsoas.
d. Pectineus.

133. If a runner injures their biceps femoris, what will they likely be unable to do?

a. Flex their arm.
b. Flex their knee.
c. Flex their wrist.
d. Flex their foot.

134. Which of the following is not found in a long bone of an adult?

a. Diaphysis.
b. Epiphysis.
c. Epiphyseal plate.
d. Yellow marrow.

135. Which of the following is a bony landmark characterized by its large, round projection?

a. Trochanter.
b. Tuberosity.
c. Tubercle.
d. Crest.

136. Which of the following is not a function of the bones?

a. Support.
b. Protection.
c. Neutralizer.
d. Movement.

137. What type of movement is someone doing if they begin in the anatomical position and move their forearms so their palms are facing toward the back?

a. Supination.
b. Pronation.
c. Retraction.
d. Inversion.

138. What type of response is seen from muscle fibers?

a. Threshold.
b. All-or-None.
c. Prime.
d. Antagonist.

139. Which of the following is not a major section of the brain?

a. Cerebrum.
b. Cerebellum.
c. Diencephalon.
d. Spinal cord.

140. How many pairs of cranial nerves are in the human body?

a. 10.
b. 11.
c. 12.
d. 13.

141. Which sensory receptors are located in the muscles, tendons, and joints?

a. Superficial.
b. Deep.
c. Visceral.
d. Pain.

142. What tissue does the antidiuretic hormone target?

a. Kidney.
b. Uterus.
c. Epithelial.
d. Thyroid.

143. Which hormone is produced in the adrenal medulla?

a. Parathyroid hormone.
b. Epinephrine.
c. Aldosterone.
d. Cortisol.

144. Which of the following is the fluid portion of blood?

a. Interstitial.
b. Intracellular.
c. Plasma.
d. Hemoglobin.

145. What can a massage therapist do to ensure they receive all necessary information from a client?

a. Have intake forms for the clients.
b. Request medical history.
c. Ask the client a couple of questions.
d. Assume that patients will tell them of any major conditions.

146. In which of the following cases would conduction occur?

a. Stone massage.
b. Sauna.
c. Using an ultrasound.
d. Warming the massage room.

147. What hydrotherapy technique may be used to treat the pelvic region only?

a. Whirlpool bath.
b. Sitz bath.
c. Ice packs.
d. Alcohol rub.

148. What is one of the most important skills a massage therapist must have for interviewing clients and general communication?

a. Remembering everything the clients says.
b. Reassuring the client massage will help.
c. Active listening.
d. Writing things down.

Answer Key and Explanations

1. A: The Integumentary system, also known as the skin, accounts for approximately 16% of the human body. In the average adult, the skin alone weighs approximately 20 pounds. While this system is also referred to as the skin, it is important to note that the hair, nails, and sweat and oil glands are also included in this system. Within this system, particularly in the skin, lie sense organs that allow a person to feel temperature, pain, and pressure. This main function of the Integumentary system is to provide protection to the other organs and tissues in the body, as well as to serve as temperature regulator and a means to synthesize various chemicals.

2. B: The Skeletal system is composed of 206 bones that provide the structure and support for the human body. In addition to the bones, within this system are tissue, cartilage, and ligaments that provide the connections and support for the bones themselves. Within the skeletal system, there are two main parts, which include the axial skeleton and the appendicular skeleton. The Axial skeleton includes the bones of the skull, the ribs, and the neck and spine. The appendicular skeleton includes the bones in the shoulder, arm and hands, pelvis, legs, and feet. These two divisions of the skeletal system are attached at the pectoral girdle, the group including the scapula and the clavicle.

3. D: The Muscular system is made up of three different muscle types including the smooth muscles, cardiac muscles, and voluntary muscles. The smooth muscles also referred to as involuntary muscles can be found in the colon, stomach, and eyes. These muscles work constantly and do not require conscious thought to perform. Voluntary muscles also referred to as skeletal muscles, take conscious effort in order to be put into action. These muscles are found on the skeleton and assist in movement. Cardiac muscles are found in the heart and are involuntary.

4. C: The nervous system includes the brain, spinal cord, and the nerves. This system serves a number of functions including communication from the brain to the body, control, and integration. All processes completed by the nervous system are completed through nerve impulses that move quickly through the body to the brain, relaying various messages. These messages will depend on which stimuli are present. For example, if you touch something hot, the nerves in your hand will relay a message to the brain based on the stimuli, the brain will process and response by sending nerve impulses back to the hand, telling the hand that it is hot.

5. D: The Endocrine system functions much like the nervous system in that it communicates, integrates, and controls. The way this system accomplishes these functions is by secreting hormones throughout the body through a series of ducts and glands. Some of the main activities the endocrine system controls and regulates include growth, metabolism, reproduction, etc. Glands within this system are dustless and are located throughout the body. For examples, in the brain are the pituitary gland and the hypothalamus, in the neck are the thyroid and the parathyroid glands, the thymus gland in the thoracic cavity, and just below in the abdominal cavity are the adrenal glands and the pancreas.

6. C: The Cardiovascular system is made up of the heart, arteries, veins, and capillaries that transport nutrients, oxygen, carbon dioxide, and waste through the blood to all sections of the body. This closed-circuit system also serves to regulate body temperature and some specialized cells of the cardiovascular system assist with the immune system. Also called the circulatory system, blood travels through the heart, leaving it by way of arteries and continues through the arterioles, capillaries, venules, and veins. The blood then returns to the heart through veins. In addition to this systemic circulation, pulmonary circulation is the process for transporting blood to the lungs;

hepatic portal circulation transports blood through the liver, and fetal circulation transports blood to and from a fetus.

7. A: The Lymphatic system transports lymph and is composed of the lymph nodes, lymphatic vessels, and other lymphatic organs such as the tonsils, spleen, and the thymus gland. Lymph contains various fatty molecules, proteins, and lymphocytes. It must be noted that there are no red blood cells within the Lymphatic system. While the lymph is transported through its own lymphatic vessels, this material will eventually travel through ducts in to the main blood stream. Two common areas in the body where lymph can be found include the armpit and the groin, were there are large collections of lymph nodes.

8. B: The Urinary system is composed of the kidneys, ureters, the bladder, and the urethra. Within this system, it is the kidney's role to clear the blood that is transported into this organ. This blood, before it is cleaned, contains waste from metabolized food. Once waste, or urine, is produced in the kidneys, it travels out of this organ in to the ureters and is stored in the bladder. As the urine leaves the body it will flow from the bladder through the urethra. Other organs that serve to rid the body of waste include the intestines, skin, and lungs.

9. C: The Respiratory system rids the body of carbon dioxide. Within the system are the nose, pharynx, larynx, trachea, bronchi, and the lungs. This system can be further broken down in to the upper respiratory system (nose, pharynx, and larynx) and the lower respiratory system (trachea, bronchi, and the lungs). Air enters the respiratory system through the nose travels through the pharynx in to the larynx to the trachea and the bronchi into the lungs, into alveoli. Alveoli are small, thin sacs where oxygen is exchanged for carbon dioxide and the carbon dioxide leaves the body. In cold climates, the air is warmed in the upper respiratory system.

10. D: The Digestive or gastrointestinal system included the teeth and the pharynx. Additionally, this system includes the mouth, esophagus, stomach, small intestine, large intestine, rectum, anal canal, salivary glands, tongue, live, gallbladder, pancreas and the appendix. This system is divided in to two groups, which include primary organs (mouth, esophagus, pharynx, stomach, small intestine, large intestine, rectum, anal canal) and accessory organs (teeth, salivary glands, tongue, live, gallbladder, pancreas, and the appendix). As food passes through the digestive tract, important nutrients will be absorbed by the body and the remaining will exit the body as waste product.

11. B: The penis and the scrotum make up the male genitalia in the male reproductive system. Within this system, the genitalia are considered supporting organs. Additionally, in the male reproductive system the gonads, or testes, are responsible for sperm production. The vas deferens and the prostate also act as accessory organs in the process of reproduction. During reproduction, the sperm travels from the testes through the vas deferens and other genital ducts through the urethra and out of the body. In this process, the prostate is responsible for producing nutrient-filled fluid that assists in reproduction.

12. A: Within the female reproductive system, the ovaries are the female gonads. Eggs are produced in the ovaries and travel through the fallopian tubes and will attach to the wall of the uterus if fertilized. Other organs in the female reproductive system include the vagina, vulva, and the mammary glands. The vagina is a tube approximately 10-cm long and is composed of involuntary muscle. It is located in between the balder and the rectum in the pelvic cavity. The vagina is also referred to as the birth canal. The vulva is the external female genitalia. Finally the mammary glands, located in the breast, are also considered external sex organs.

13. A: The Craniosacral division is the nerves of the parasympathetic division that lead off from the cranial and the sacral segments of the spinal cord. This system results in an opposite response to the sympathetic systems, and includes the contraction of the pupils and the return to a normal heart rate. In addition to these effects, the craniosacral system as a whole has an impulse called the craniosacral impulse. This impulse can be palpated through slow and steady body work. The impulse is the rhythm of the individual's body and will vary from person to person.

14. B: Serous membranes are found in the closed cavities of the body. This type of membrane is classified as an epithelial membrane and is made up of two layers. This top layer is the squamous epithelium and the bottom layer is connective tissues called the basement membrane. Additionally, these membranes are named according to where in the body they are located and what they cover, and more specifically, when covering the wall of a cavity it is termed a parietal portion and when covering an organ this membrane is termed the visceral portion. Serous membranes within the thoracic cavity are referred to as pleura, and those within the abdominal cavity are referred to at peritoneum. Therefore, the serous membrane that covers the wall of the abdominal cavity is called the parietal peritoneum, covering the organs within the abdominal cavity referred to as the visceral peritoneum. Those covering the lining of the thoracic cavity are referred to as the parietal pleura, whereas those covering the organs within the thoracic cavity are called visceral pleura.

15. B: The width of the epiphyseal plate can provide information for an estimate of the adult height of an individual. The epiphyseal plate is located between the epiphyses and the diaphysis within bone and as children, this is a cartilage substance. This estimate may be made when the individual is a child, prior to ossification. A common technique for this estimation is obtaining an x-ray of a child's bones, often the wrist, and determining if and how much of the epiphyseal plate is cartilage. As the child grows, this plate will completely transform into bone, at which point the individual will stop growing.

16. A: As a muscle moves, the synergist provides support to the prime mover. Both the synergist and the prime mover muscles contract while the antagonist muscles relax. Therefore, the movement of pulling your forearm up requires your biceps brachii to be the prime movers and the bicep brachialis serve as the synergists. The triceps are the antagonist of the movement because they are required to relax in order to stretch out. As the forearm is moved back down in a straight position, the role of these muscles is reversed and the triceps become the prime movers and the biceps brachii the antagonists.

17. D: Sensory neurons provide information to the brain from various parts of the body. This type of neuron is also referred to as afferent neurons. Motor neurons, also referred to as efferent neurons, send signals and information from the brain to either muscle or glandular epithelial tissue. These neurons send signals that tell the various parts of the body what to do. Interneurons act as connecting neurons as they send information from the motor neurons to the sensory neurons. Together, these three types of neurons create a loop-type system of information transfer. As an example of this process, if an individual touches something hot, that information will be sent up to the brain through the sensory neurons; once the brain processes the information, it is sent back through motor neurons. The interneurons come into play when information must be passed from the sensory to the motor neurons and vice versa.

18. C: The second messenger mechanism is the main mechanism of functioning for nonsteroid hormones. For this process, a first messenger is required; commonly a protein hormone which will attach to a specific receptor site on the cell membrane. Once the connection between the protein hormone and the cell receptor site has been accomplished, chemical reaction occurs and activates the second messengers, which are in the cell. Once the second messengers are activated, then the hormone can carry out its specific function. This process is a form of communication between the hormones and the cells. A common example of this process can be demonstrated by the hormone adenosine monophosphate, which is a second messenger that provides the cell with necessary information for activity.

19. A: The tunica externa is the outermost layer of both an artery and a vein, and is thinner in arteries. This layer is composted of connective tissue, and its primary function is that of support and reinforcement of the artery or vein to prevent bursting under the pressure of blood flow. In addition to this layer, arteries and veins also have a tunica media, responsible for the regulation of blood pressure, and tunica intima, a smooth film lining arteries and veins that prevents unintentional blood clotting. Unique to veins are the semilunar valves located within the tunica intima. These valves prevent backflow of blood as it travels back to the heart.

20. B: Approximately 75% of the body dumps its lymph into the thoracic duct. The thoracic duct is located on the left subclavian vein and is the largest lymphatic vessel in the body. Lymph for all parts of the body except the upper right extremity flows through the thoracic duct. In addition to the thoracic duct, the right lymphatic duct is located on the right subclavian vein. Lymph from the right sides of the head, neck, chest, and right arm enter into the right lymphatic duct. All lymph flows in one direction and eventually enters back into the blood stream to be discarded as waste. Additionally, a structure in the abdomen, called the cistern chili, acts as a storage area for lymph traveling toward the thoracic duct.

21. B: The respiratory membrane acts to separate air into the alveoli, or the blood in the capillaries. This membrane can be found lining the wall of the alveoli, which are small sacs that fill with air located at the end of the bronchioles. The respiratory membrane consists of various layers including the alveolar wall, interstitial fluid, and the pulmonary capillary wall. The alveolar wall is comprised of epithelial cells, while the pulmonary capillary wall is made up of endothelial cells. The process of oxygen and carbon dioxide travelling across the respiratory membrane is diffusion.

22. C: Digestion begins in the mouth with the teeth. The teeth serve digestion by breaking food down for further processing. While the mouth is considered a main organ within the digestive system, the teeth are accessory organs. The tongue, also an accessory organ, assists the teeth in this initial breakdown of food. From the mouth, food will travel down the pharynx to the esophagus, then to the stomach, the small intestine, the large intestine, the rectum, and finally the anal canal. As the food moves through this system, various chemical reactions occur and food is metabolized as essential nutrients are removed and distributed or stored in the body as needed.

23. D: Cerebrospinal fluid is manipulated during a craniosacral therapeutic session. This fluid can be found between the dura mater, the arachnoid membrane, and the pia mater. These three layers of membrane make up the meningeal system. More specifically, the dura mater is the outermost membrane and functions as waterproof protection. The arachnoid membrane is the middle layer, and provides the necessary lubrication for the outer- and innermost membranes of this system to easily glide. Finally, the pia mater is the innermost membrane that lines the brain and spinal cord. Because the cerebrospinal fluid serves as lubrication between these membrane layers, if this fluid is not flowing freely through the craniosacral system, then pain may result.

24. A: With the process of resorption, fluid moves from the renal tubules into the blood stream. Common substances that undergo the process of resorption include water, proteins, sodium, and other essential nutrients. Resorption begins at the proximal convoluted tubules through the loop of Henle, through the distal convoluted tubules and into the collecting tubules. Resorption occurs through osmosis, and nearly 99% of water is resorbed on a daily basis. Additionally, one nutrient, glucose, is also resorbed. The body's inability to resorb glucose results in a condition referred to as glycosuria, or glucose in the urine, which is a sign of diabetes mellitus.

25. A: The Anatomical Position, according to western medicine, is achieved when the body standing erect with hands at the sides and palms facing forward. In addition, the head and feet also face forward. This universal position allows communication between professionals in the healthcare industry. Using the anatomical position as a reference point, we are able to discuss and locate various parts of the body. In terms of referencing the body using this position, anatomical directions include superior (toward the head) and inferior (away from the head); anterior (front) and posterior (back); medial (toward the midline) and lateral (toward the side); proximal (toward the trunk) and distal (away from the trunk); and superficial (near the surface) and deep (away from the surface).

26. D: The midsagittal is the plane that goes from top to bottom, which divides the body in left and right sides directly in the middle. This should not be confused with the sagittal plane, which divides the body in left and right sides but does not do so directly down the middle of the body or organ. Other planes that are used to determine and discuss a specific location of the body include frontal, running side to side and dividing the body into front and back, and transverse, running horizontally, dividing the body into top and bottom.

27. D: None of the above. The abdominopelvic cavity and the thoracic cavity are divisions of the ventral cavity. The lungs are contained within the thoracic cavity. The dorsal cavity consists of the cranial cavity and spinal canal.

28. C: The semimembranosus is not a major muscle of the head, but is in fact a muscle of the hamstring group, with an insertion at the tibia and origin at the ischium and functions to flex the knee. The Orbicularis oculi is located above the eye, with an insertion and origin at the maxilla and functions to closes the eye. The Zygomaticus is located at the cheek with an insertion at the angle of the mouth and upper lip and an origin at the Zygomatic arch and functions to elevate the corners of the mouth. Finally, the Masseter is located at the jaw with an insertion at the mandible and an origin at the Zygomatic arch and functions to close the mouth.

29. C: The trapezius has an origin at the external occipital protuberance ligamentum nuchae and an insertion at the lateral third of clavicle acromion. The trapezius also has an origin at the C7-T12 spinous process and two additional insertions at the spine of the scapula and the root of the spine of the scapula. The trapezius is a triangular shaped muscle and is the most superficial muscle in the back. The action of the trapezius is elevation and upward rotation of the scapula, and retraction of the scapula. This muscle lies superior to the latissimus dorsi, and the teres major and minor.

30. B: The latissimus dorsi has an action of medial rotation and adduction of the humerus. This muscle also has an origin at the thoracolumbar aponeurosis, the lower six thoracic spinous processes, the iliac crest and the sacrum, the lower 4 ribs, and the inferior angle of the scapula. The insertion of the latissimus dorsi is at the bicipital groove of the humerus. This muscle is the widest muscle in the back and is very useful for activities that require a lot of power such as swimming. In addition to the action of rotation, the latissimus dorsi is responsible for extension.

31. C: The lower trapezius is depressor of the scapula.

32. D: An isometric contraction occurs when a muscle contracts but no movement is produced. Isometric is a Greek word meaning "equal measure." As it pertains to muscle movement and contraction, if a muscle shortens, then it will move. However, in this type of muscle contraction the length in the relaxed state is the same, or equal to the length of the muscle in the contracted state.

What is occurring within the muscle during an isometric contraction is that the muscle tension increases. This type of contraction can be accomplished by pushing or pulling on a stationary object.

33. A: A twitch contraction is an involuntary, quick movement. This type of muscle contraction typically occurs in response to a stimulus; for example, a fly landing on your arm or touching something too hot or too cold. Research on muscle contractions such as twitches has been able to isolate individual muscles and cause these individual muscle fibers to twitch. However, in real-life movements, a twitch will not occur on an isolated muscle fiber due to the all-or-none response. This muscle response is one in which either all the fibers of a muscle move, or none of them move.

34. B: The origin is the muscle attachment on the more stationary bone. Every muscle will have an origin and there are a number of muscles that have more than one origin. The tendons, on the other hand, are tissue that connects the muscle to the bone. Tendons will be found at both the insertion and the origin of the muscle. The insertion is the part of the muscle that is attached on the more movable part. Finally the bursae are sacs filled with fluid located between the tendon and the bone. These fluid-filled sacs help with movement by providing a lubricant called the synovial fluid.

35. B: Tendons anchor the muscle to the bone. Tendons are made up of dense connective tissue so that the muscle firmly attaches to bone. Tendons are further protected by tendon sheaths. These tendon sheaths are lined with a synovial membrane that provides lubrication to the tendon in order to allow for easy movement. The bursae can be found between some tendons and the bone and serve to provide lubrication to decrease friction between the tendon and bone. Without the tendon sheaths and the bursae, movement would be painful and very difficult, because the tendons would not be able to easily move, and the friction between the bone and the tendon would result in tearing.

36. C: The iliopsoas and the adductor muscles serve to move the lower extremities. Specifically, the iliopsoas has an origin at the ilium and vertebrae and an insertion at the femur. This muscle flexes the thigh and the trunk of the body. Other muscles that move the thigh or the trunk of the body include the sartorius (flexes thigh and rotates legs) and the gluteus maximus (extends thigh). The adductor muscles are a group that includes the adductor longus, gracilis, and the pectineus, all of which adduct the thigh. All three adductor muscles have an origin at the pubis, while the adductor longus and pectineus have an insertion at the femur and the gracilis has an insertion at the tibia.

37. C: The orbicularis oculi closes the eyes. This muscle has an origin and insertion at the maxilla and the frontal bone, and therefore circles the eye. Another muscle that moves the eyes is the frontal muscle with an origin at the occipital bone and insertion at the eyebrow, this muscle raises the eyebrows. The muscles that move the eyes are important for facial expressions. While these muscles move the eye brows and eye lids, there are a number of muscles in the skull that move the eyeball itself. These include the medial, lateral, superior, and inferior rectus muscles, and the superior and inferior oblique muscles.

38. A: The skull contains synarthroses joints, also referred to as suture because of the suture-like appearance. In newborns these joints are not fully formed, resulting in the soft spot on the top of the head which is fibrous tissue. As the child grows, the bones close. These joints are immobile because connective tissue has grown between the bones. While synarthroses joints are often discussed in terms of having mo movement, those in the skull do have slight movement caused by the ebb and flow of spinocranial fluid. In craniosacral therapy, the bones in the skull are palpated and the therapist can feel the movement of these bones.

39. C: Diarthrosis joints are the most common type of joint in the human body. These joints move freely. All diarthrosis joints have three common structures, which include the joint capsule, joint cavity, and cartilage covering the ends of the two adjoining bones. These structures are made up of connective tissues and synovial membranes that allow the joint to move in one or more directions. The type of movement a diarthrosis joint has will depend on its location within the body and the specific joint type. Joint types include ball and socket, hinge, pivot, saddle, gliding, and condyloid.

40. A: The joint in the shoulder is a ball and socket joint. This type of joint allows full movement of the shoulder which includes side to side, up and down, and in a circular motion. With ball and socket joints, the end of one bone is shaped like a ball and the end of the other bones is a concave, cup-like shape. These two bones fit snuggly together with a synovial membrane separating them to reduce friction and allow easy movement. When a joint is "popped out of socket" this is referring to this ball and socket joint, when the ball end comes out of the socket end.

41. B: Neurologists use dermatomes to determine the exact location of a spinal injury. Dermatomes refer to specific locations on the skin surface that are connected to only one nerve. Looking at a dermatome map of the body, one can see that the skin surface is divided into 5 segments, or dermatomes; cervical, thoracic, lumbar, sacral, and coccygeal. Within each of these segments are further divisions or layers that connect to a specific nerve. More specifically, there are 8 cervical, 12 thoracic, 5 lumbar, 5 sacral, and one coccygeal nerve; therefore each segment has the corresponding subdivisions.

42. C: There are 12 primary meridians in the human body including the lung, colon, stomach, spleen, heart, intestine, triple warmer, pericardium, urinary bladder, kidney, gallbladder, and liver meridians. Each point of these meridians corresponds to a location, function, and time in the body, and all primary meridians correspond to an internal organ. In oriental medicine, meridians carry the flow of Qi to all parts of the body. The flow of Qi is as follows: note the time in parentheses refers to the time of activity for that organ: lungs (3:00 AM-5:00 AM), large intestine (5:00 AM-7:00 AM), stomach (7:00 AM-9:00 AM), spleen (9:00 AM-11:00 AM), heart (11:00 AM-1:00 PM), small intestine (1:00 PM-3:00 PM), urinary bladder (3:00 PM-5:00 PM), kidney (5:00 PM-7:00 PM), pericardium (7:00 PM-9:00 PM), triple warmer (9:00 PM-11:00 PM), gallbladder (11:00 PM-1:00 AM), and liver (1:00 AM-3:00 AM).

43. C: Stress is the condition in which the body is not in balance. Stressors on the body can range and include physical or mental stimuli. During stress glucocorticoid production and release is increased by the adrenal cortex. This process is the first step in the stress response. Once glucocorticoid concentrations are elevated in the body, there is an increase in the amount of fats and proteins that are metabolized atrophy in the thymus, and the inflammatory response becomes inhibited. From here other stress responses are put into action until the body once again reaches homeostasis, or balance.

44. B: Cushing syndrome typically results from a hypersecretion of glucocorticoids. This syndrome is characterized by physical abnormalities such as moon-face and buffalo hump. These abnormalities are cause because of an abnormal redistribution of fat causing the face or upper back, respectively to be larger and more rounded than normal. Another common symptom of this syndrome is an increased production of testosterone leading to the appearance of male secondary sexual characteristics. This syndrome is more common in women and individuals with Cushing have higher than normal blood sugar levels and frequent infections. The physical abnormalities of this syndrome can be corrected with surgery.

45. A: Carbohydrate loading would be the most beneficial nutritional practice or technique for an individual preparing for a marathon. Carbohydrate loading is the intake of a large amount of carbohydrates for storage in the body, specifically, in skeletal muscle fibers. When athletes consume a high carbohydrate diet, they are able to store up to two times as many carbohydrates as normal. This additional energy will allow them to sustain physical activity for a longer period. As energy is needed, the body takes the stored carbohydrates and processes them through glucose catabolism, which has three stages: (1) glycolysis; (2) citric acid cycle; and (3) electron transfer system.

46. C: Muscle contraction requires energy or ATP molecules. With a muscle contraction, all parts of the muscle are involved, otherwise known as an all-or-nothing response. Specifically, the muscle is composed of fibers with thick and thin myofilaments that produce proteins, myosin and actin, respectively, upon contraction. The action of a contracting muscle can be observed by looking at the sarcomeres. As the muscle contrasts, the distance between the z-lines of the sarcomeres shortens, whereas when the muscle relaxes, the distance increases. Thick and thin myofilaments slide toward each other, overlapping during muscle contraction. This is also referred to as the sliding filament model.

47. C: In a tonic contraction, there is no muscle movement. However, the muscles do serve to support the body. A tonic contraction will occur anytime an individual is in an upright position. Another way to describe this type of contraction is posture. Individuals with good posture have strong muscles that are also properly aligned with other parts of the body; the opposite is true for individuals with poor posture. The muscles specifically involved in maintaining posture are back and neck muscles, because gravity tends to pull the head and trunk of the body down.

48. A: Flexion occurs when there is a decrease in the angle between two bones. In addition to the decrease in the angle, during flexion, there is a decrease in the length of the prime mover and an increase in the length of the antagonist associated with the bones. In this example, when the angle between the forearm and the humorous decreases, the length of the bicep decreases while the triceps increase in length. Similar to flexing the arm, one can also flex the leg in which one would bend the leg back at the knee, shortening the hamstring muscle group and lengthening the quadriceps.

49. C: Abduction is a movement away from the midline. By moving your arms straight out to the sides and away from the midline, you are abducting your arms. Muscles involved in this type of movement include the deltoid as the prime mover and rotator cuff muscles as the synergists. In order for abduction to occur, the deltoid must contract. Additionally, the glenohumeral joint is also involved. The opposite movement to abduction is adduction. Adduction is the movement toward the midline. When you bring your arms back down to your body, adduction occurs.

50. D: Plantar flexion results in the toes pointing downward. Plantar flexion is also required to move into a position where you are standing on your toes. This movement will increase the degree of the angle between the top of the foot and the ankle. The primary muscles involved in plantar flexion include the gastrocnemius, soleus, plantaris, flexor hallucis longus, flexor digitorum longus, and the tibialis posterior. The lateral muscles involved in this movement include the peroneus longus and peroneus brevis. The opposite movement is dorsiflexion, which results in the toes pointing upward and decreased the degree of the angle between the top of the foot and the ankle.

51. A: Rotation is the movement that occurs when shaking your head "no." This movement occurs around a longitudinal axis. The main joint type in the neck that allows this movement is a condyloid joint. Other types of rotation include internal rotation, also referred to as media rotation. Internal rotation is a rotation toward the midline. For example, you can rotate your shoulder or hip toward your midline. External rotation, or lateral rotation, is the movement of rotation away from the midline. Rotating your hip out so your toes point away from the midline is an example of external rotation.

52. C: Proprioceptors are receptors found between tendons and muscles as well as deep within the skeleton that provide the brain with information about body position or movement. These receptors are enclosed. When there is trauma to a proprioceptor, it could result in permanent damage, leading to the loss of feeling of the muscles. Two important proprioceptors include the Golgi tendons and muscle spindles. Golgi tendons are located at the junction of tendons and muscles and detect tension the muscle. Muscle spindles located in all skeletal muscles detect the length of a muscle.

53. B: Receptors are often distinguished by whether or not they are encapsulated (covered) or unencapsulated (free or naked). There are six main encapsulated receptors. Meissner's corpuscles located on the skin, fingertips, and lips and detect very fine touches and low frequency vibrations. Ruffini's corpuscles are also located at the dermal layer of the skin and the subcutaneous tissues of the fingers and detect both touch and pressure. The Pacinian corpuscles are located at various levels of tissues at joints, the mammary glands, and external genitalia and detect pressure and high frequency vibrations. Krause's end-bulbs are located in the skin, lips, eyelids, and external genitalia and detect touch and cold. Golgi tendons and muscle spindles, located in skeletal muscles detect muscle tension and length.

54. C: Anorexia is an illness in which the individual starves themselves. In these cases the body will compensate for the lack of nutrients and use up all available resources. This begins with the use of all stored fat throughout the body. Following this, the body will begin to use up its protein stores in order to provide itself with energy. During this process, the protein molecules will go through catabolism and the amino acids making up these proteins will be broken down and converted into glucose which then begins the citric acid cycle. Because the body needs proteins for survival, when the body uses these proteins solely for energy, death may occur.

55. A: An individual with a vitamin C deficiency may develop scurvy. Scurvy is characterized by the inability to make and maintain collagen fibers which is necessary for connective tissues. Common physical symptoms of scurvy include skin spots, spongy gums, and bleeding. Prior to modern day technologies and knowledge about the importance of vitamins, this disease was very common among sailors who may not have had efficient access to the fruits and vegetables that provide vitamin C. While if untreated, scurvy can be fatal, individuals with this disease can make full recoveries with the intake of vitamin C.

56. D: Copper is an essential mineral. Individuals deficient in copper may experience fatigue and anemia. Adequate amounts of copper can be found in seafood, organ meats, and legumes. Copper's primary function in the body with regard to metabolism is to extract energy from the citric acid cycle of catabolism as well as during the production of blood. In addition to these functions, copper also serves to provide the blood with oxygen and maintain healthy hair color. While copper can be obtained from various foods, the body is also able to absorb copper through the skin and many individuals have found wearing copper jewelry, particularly bracelets, beneficial for ailments such as arthritis.

57. D: Protein-calorie malnutrition, also referred to as PCM, is a deficiency in calories and protein in particular. This disorder is typically the result of an individual eating less; however, it can also occur if the body begins to use up more nutrients than normal. This type of malnutrition is often seen in mild form during most illnesses. More extreme cases of this type of malnutrition can be seen in various disorders. For example, those disorders that cause a reduced nutrient intake include: anorexia, self-induced starvation; dysphagia, inability or difficulty swallowing; gastrointestinal obstructions; and nausea. Disorders that result in the loss of nutrients include diarrhea; glycosuria, glucose in the urine; and hemorrhage. Finally, those that cause the body to use more nutrients than normal include burns, fever, and infection.

58. A: The descending colon is likely to be affected when a patient complains of pain in the left lumbar region. The abdominopelvic cavity is divided in to four regions: Right upper, Left upper, Right lower, and Left lower. Within these regions the abdominopelvic cavity is further divided in to nine sections. By dividing this cavity into sections, healthcare workers are also to communicate clearly about a patient. With regard to the nine sections, these include the right hypochondriac region, epigastric region, left hypochondriac region, Right lumbar region, umbilical region, left lumbar region, Right iliac region, hypogastric region, and the left iliac region.

59. B: The feedback loop is the primary function that maintains homeostasis in the human body. This feedback loop detects when the body is unbalanced and triggers the appropriate mechanisms to bring it back into balance, much like the principles of input and output seen in engineering. Essentially, the nerve endings are the sensors that send messages to the brain, or control center, where the information is processed and acted upon. For example, on a cold day, the skin senses the cold temperature, sends this information to the brain; and the brain tells the muscles (effectors) to shiver, thus bringing the body temperature up. When the body temperature is at the appropriate level, the shivering will stop.

60. C: The plasma membrane's structure is a phospholipid bilayer with proteins. This part of the cell serves as a barrier and protects the cell. On the outer surface of this membrane, protein and carbohydrates have the function of markers to differentiate cells from one another. These components also serve to identify various receptor cells for hormones that will only act on specific cells. The plasma membrane is approximately seven nanometers thick and in addition to protecting the cell, this membrane keeps the cell together with the layers of phospholipid as well as cholesterol that helps stabilize the phospholipids.

61. A: A paper cut will damage the epithelial tissue. Epithelial tissue covers the outside of the body and is a protective barrier. This type of tissue also covers the cavities within the body. The cells of epithelial tissues are packed closely together and cell division is rapid. There are three types of epithelial tissue, cutaneous membrane, serous membrane, and mucous membrane. Cutaneous membranes are the most visible and most abundant in the body, as this type of tissue makes up the skin. Serous membranes are located within closed cavities and have two layers, an epithelial sheet and a layer of simple squamous epithelium. Finally, the mucous membranes are located in cavities that open to the exterior, for example, in the respiratory organs.

62. C: The epiphyseal plate will be the part of the bone that a doctor will look at to determine the adult height of an individual. This structure is made of cartilage and is located between the epiphysis and the diaphysis of the long bone. As the child grows, the epiphyseal plate will begin to harden and when all of the cartilage is harden into bone, growth stops. Once growth stops, what is left is the epiphyseal line marking the point where the epiphysis and the diaphysis have joined. Height can be determined by the thickness of the cartilage, typically by x-raying the wrist.

63. B: The sympathetic system is responsible for responding in emergency situations. This system is a part of the larger autonomic nervous system and is also referred to as the thoracolumbar division. This is often referred to as the fight or flight response. During these situations the sympathetic system will cause a number of other systems or responses to go at the same time. This increased activation of responses allows the body the energy necessary to deal with the stressful situation. Examples of increased responses include sweating, increased heart rate, and secretion of epinephrine, a hormone of the adrenal medulla that reinforces the effects of norepinephrine.

64. C: The muscle pattern that causes the rippled look of a toned stomach is called strap. With this pattern the muscle fibers are aligned and parallel. Other muscle patterns are pinnate, bipennate, multipennate, and triangular, in which fibers are in a diagonal pattern. A fusiform pattern is one in which the fibers are parallel in the belly of the muscle. Spiral and tricipital fibers are twisted and have three muscle bellies, respectively. These patterns are clearly visible and will vary depending on the muscle and its function. For example, the deltoids have a multipennate pattern; the trapezius has a triangular pattern; and the latissimus dorsi has a spiral pattern.

65. D: The possible sprain is contraindicated for massage until a doctor has examined the injury. A sprain can be a stretch, tear, or rip of muscle and can be any one of three grades, or degree of injury. With a mild sprain, Grade 1, the pain is local and tension in the muscle is increased. A moderate or Grade 2 sprain will show indications of reduced or impaired muscle function. With a severe or Grade 3 sprain, there is typically loss of muscle function. It is important to be aware of possible injuries a client may have recently sustained, and while gentle massage may be indicated for such injuries, always have a doctor examine the injury first.

66. B: The most common term in the medical field would be fibromyalgia. It is important for the massage therapist to know and understand medical terminology because it is the key to understanding the body and its pathology. This terminology is the means to speak a common language, which is familiar to all healthcare professionals. Miscommunications in terminology can lead to misunderstandings or more severe consequences to the patient. Understanding medical terminology will also help the therapist when writing treatment notes. When learning medical terminology, consider the parts of the word, for example, Fibro-, meaning fiber or fibrous and my-, meaning muscle. Knowing this we know that the term fibromyalgia is referring to the fibrous muscle tissue. The suffix, -algia means pain. Therefore, when a client states they have fibromyalgia, the therapist will know to be cautious not to cause more pain during the massage.

67. A: Cysts on the kidneys is a symptom rather than a part of the disease's etiology. The definition of etiology is then the incidence or situation in which a disease may occur. In this example, polycystic kidney disease is often hereditary with most cases exhibiting a mutation of the PKD1 gene. Additionally, research suggests that approximately 5% of patients with polycystic kidney disease are in end-stage renal disease. The etiology of a disease will vary depending on the disease, and may include anything from genetics to environmental causes. For example, emphysema, a respiratory disease, may have an etiology of environmental causes.

68. A: Tuberculosis is an airborne illness, meaning the disease is spread through the air, especially when an individual with the disease coughs or sneezes. For contagious diseases, there are a number of ways that the disease can be transmitted: through the air, blood, saliva, or sexual fluids. In order to prevent the healthcare workers from acquiring the disease, they must wear a mask. Blood-borne diseases may be spread through IV drug use, blood transfusions, or cuts. For a massage therapist, the best way to protect themselves from these types of illnesses is to be cautious and aware any cuts on their hands. If cuts or openings are present, then they should either wait until the cut is healed to massage or wear gloves.

69. B: Signs can be observed and measured. Coughing blood, fever, chills, and weight loss, all can be seen by outside observers and measures. On the other hand, chest pain would be referred to as a symptom, which is something that is subjective and only felt by the patient. Diseases contain both signs and symptoms and these words are often used interchangeably. As a massage therapist, you will never diagnose an individual, however if someone complains to you about various symptoms or you see signs that are questionable, you can also suggest they see their primary care physician.

70. A: Massage releases serotonin as well as dopamine. The release of serotonin regulates moods and allows the appropriate emotions to be displayed during any specific situation. Serotonin also effects in the individual in terms of calming. In an individual with depression, their serotonin is low. When serotonin is released, it may level out the depressed mood. Other psychological issues such as obsessive-compulsive disorders, chronic pain disorders, and eating disorders are also indicated by lower levels of serotonin, and may therefore benefit from massage. It is always important for a massage therapist to be aware of psychological problems and medication their clients are on, as some have adverse reactions to a calming massage.

71. C: The most appropriate massage technique for individuals with autism would be a firm, purposeful touch. These individuals, while some would think counter-intuitively, do like and want to be touched. However, for individuals with autism, their development disability is one in which social interactions are hindered and their days consist of a series of deliberate actions and behaviors. Therefore, massage should also be as such in order to make the client feel comfortable. Most importantly, a massage therapist must always respect the client and remain in constant communication during the massage, to ensure they are having a comfortable and beneficial experience.

72. A: Massage in general will influence the automatic nervous system and in a relaxation massage, this can be very calming, thus reducing the amount of anxiety felt by the client. Massage therapists must always remember to begin with a client based on where they are personally. For example, if a client comes into a massage with heightened anxiety, they may be resistant to gentle slow strokes at first. Therefore, the therapist should communicate with and respect the client in order to create a massage that is beneficial for them and helps ease their anxiety.

73. A: Individuals with osteoporosis have a serious bone disease. This disease results in a loss of bone density, specifically the loss of calcium, and is most typical in postmenopausal women. While its direct cause is unknown, osteoporosis has been linked to a decrease in the female hormone estrogen. Literally translated, osteoporosis means a porous bone. In some individuals, the condition will have progressed to a point where bone fractures can occur with no or little impact. Therefore, it is important for a therapist to be aware of any condition and adjust their massage accordingly.

74. B: The informed consent is the form required that gives the therapist permission to work on an individual. This form must be signed by a consenting adult or, in the case of body work for a minor, a legal guardian. It is important that the informed consent provides information about the nature of massage as well as information indicating that the individual has the right to refuse treatment at any point during the massage. By providing clients with this information, they have the opportunity to make an educated, informed decision on whether they want to receive treatment.

75. C: Transference occurs during a client-therapist relationship when the client transfers personal feelings onto the therapist. In this case the client may be seeing you as so much like their deceased spouse that they begin feeling for you what they felt of their spouse. As a massage therapist, this issue should be dealt with professionally and with sensitivity. If the client is unable to deal with these feelings in a healthy way, it would be most responsible for the therapist to refer the client to another massage therapist and/or grief counseling so they could learn to deal with the death of their spouse.

76. D: Countertransference occurs when a therapist places personal feelings on to their client. In this case as a therapist also recently dealing with the death of a loved one, you may find that your client reminds you of the deceased. It could also be that because of the similarities in your situations you may feel a superficial connection and attribute that connection to something deep. In this case, the best solution may be to be honest with your client and refer them to a different therapist.

77. B: Massaging your client's face would be crossing their personal boundaries. Personal boundaries will be different for everyone, and it is important to learn what these boundaries are for each client before beginning a massage. These are boundaries that we all set for ourselves on how close someone can get before we are no longer comfortable. In this situation, because your client stated prior to the massage that they did not like having their face massaged, then this clearly is a personal boundary. If a massage therapist ignores these things, then the massage will become an unpleasant experience for the client. Additionally, not all clients will say out loud what their boundaries are. By paying attention and watching for signs of discomfort, a therapist can ask questions and modify the massage to make sure the client is comfortable.

78. C: Listening and offering your own assessment of your client's situation is beyond a massage therapist's scope of practices and therefore would be considered crossing a legal and ethical boundary. It is important for a massage therapist to be empathic and show concern and sensitivity, especially for clients in vulnerable positions. However, a therapist can cause unwarranted damage if they offer services that they are unqualified to provide. In situations where a therapist crosses a legal boundary, they are at risk for not only harming their clients, but also harming their practice and may face legal actions.

79. A: Medical terminology is a set of terms, typically Latin or Greek that provides all healthcare professionals a common language. While not all massage therapists will work directly with a chiropractor or other medical professional, it will still be important for all to understand and know how to properly use medical terminology. There may be times throughout your career that you encounter a client with various health needs. In some cases, a physician, or other healthcare professional consultation will be necessary in order for you to provide the best and safest care to your client.

80. C: An independent contractor essentially is their own boss. While, as an independent contractor you may rent a room from a spa, you are still responsible for paying all of your own taxes; however, the rent you pay for the room rental could be deducted as a business expense. Independent contractors must keep careful records of all of their profits and losses, as all will be included on schedule C of their tax forms. In addition to keeping records, independent contractors are required to pay quarterly taxes, which is typically one quarter of the tax you expect to owe by the end of the year.

81. B: While not required in many European countries, draping is required by law for massage in the United States. This is a way the massage therapist can maintain their client's privacy and ensure the client is comfortable and warm throughout the massage. There are various techniques for draping; however, the main focus is to uncover only the body part you are working on. As noted, draping is also used to keep the client warm. Since as the client relaxes their body temperature may decrease, it is very easy to become cold during a massage. With this additional point in mind, therapists should also have extra blankets on hand.

82. A: Endangerment sites are locations on the body where the nerves are superficial. Pressure on these areas may cause the client extreme discomfort or potential damage to the underlying vessels and nerves. In addition to the armpit, the following are also considered endangerment sites: the eyes, inferior to the ear, the posterior cervical area, lymph nodes, the medial brachium, musculocutaneous nerve, median nerve, ulnar nerve, basilic vein, cubital areas of the median nerve, and radial and ulnar arteries and under the knees. Light strokes over these areas may be allowable; however, a massage therapist must always be careful and watch for signs of discomfort.

83. C: When discussing various conditions in terms of severity, healthcare workers will typically refer to the condition as acute or chronic. In this case, the back pain is chronic because it is existed for about a year. Had the client stated that his back problems began last week, the condition would be considered acute. Acute conditions will typically be short in duration; however, if a condition continues, it can become a chronic problem. As a massage therapist, it is important to understand if a client's conditions are acute or chronic so you know how to treat and track the problem.

84. C: If a client comes for a massage and is ill, the best thing of their therapist to do would be to refer them to a physician. Referrals are necessary in some cases because the therapist is not qualified to diagnosis or treat diseases. Referrals can also be used to enhance the client's treatment and healing. For example, you may refer a client to a chiropractor and suggest they have their back adjusted immediately following a massage. This would enhance the client's healing process. Because referrals are common in this field, it is important for therapists to be familiar with the various healthcare professionals in their area.

85. A: Confidentiality is the client's right to privacy. According to the Health Insurance Portability and Accountability Act of 1996, all healthcare professionals are required to maintain their client's confidentiality, which includes all massage therapists. When a new client comes in for a massage, it is the therapist's responsibility to inform the client about confidentiality and their rights to privacy. While therapists must maintain confidentiality, there may be situations were discussing a case is allowable; for example, when consulting with other healthcare professionals, if they are discussing clients with a supervisor for training or evaluation purposes, or if required by law.

86. B: S.O.A.P refers to Subjective Objective Assessment and Plan. With this form of note taking, the therapist will provide a range of information beginning with subjective information. This will consist completely of information that the client provides to the therapist. The subjective information will be what the therapist finds after working on the client. This could include information such as range of motion or observed signs of disorder. The assessment section of the documentation will include the outcomes of the session, for medical doctors, this section would include a diagnosis. Finally, the plan section of these notes will discuss the treatment plan.

87. C: Lymphatic massage would be contraindicated by a malignant neoplasm because this is a tumor or cancer that can be spread. Such tumors are abnormal growths, often caused by genetic conditions and are registered by the rest of the body as parasites. In many cases malignant neoplasms are spread through the lymphatic system and if massage if performed, the therapists may spread this disease to other parts of the body. The other type of tumor is a benign tumor, which is not spreadable. These tumors typically grow slower then malignant tumors and only become life-threatening if they grow to a size that hinders the functioning of surrounding organs.

88. A: Sprains are injuries to ligaments and are classified in three grades. In this case, the sprain would be classified as a Grade 1 sprain, which is mild and includes 0%-20% fiber tear. With this grade, the individual will continue to have normal range of motion by the area may be tender and slightly swollen. A Grade 2 sprain refers to a 20%-75% fiber tear, moderate resistance, swelling, muscle splinting, and a reduced range of motion. The final type of sprain is a Grade 3 sprain and refers to a 75%-100% fiber tear. This is a severe sprain that is painful and little to no motion.

89. C: Strains are injuries to muscles and tendons and are classified in three degrees. A first-degree strain results in 0%-10% fiber tear, mild pain and tenderness, and swelling. With a first-degree strain, the individual usually still has all normal functioning. A second-degree strain results in a 10%-50% fiber tear, pain, swelling, muscle splinting, and a reduced functioning. Finally, a third-degree strain results in a 50%-100% fiber tear, severe pain, swelling, and little to no muscle functioning. Regardless of the degree of the strain, massage is contraindicated for at least the first 24 hours after the injury and it may be beneficial for the therapist to refer the client for further evaluation and treatment prior to massaging the strained area.

90. B: A complete fracture is one in which the bone becomes completely separated. In addition to this type of fracture, other types of fractures include incomplete, closed, open, comminuted, compression, stress, greenstick, nonunion, malunion, delayed union, and spiral fractures. Of the more common fractures, the incomplete fracture results in a crack that does not go all the way through the bone. A closed fracture affects the bone but not the skin, while an open fracture affects both the bone and skin. A comminuted fracture results in the bone being cracked or splintered in more than one piece and a compression fracture is when the bone is pushed together, resulting in a fracture.

91. D: Cervicogenic headaches are related to various trigger points and would benefit from this type of massage. Symptoms of cervicogenic headaches may include altered neck posture and a limited range of motion. Other headache types include migraine, cluster, tension, and chronic daily. Migraine headaches are severe headaches with symptoms such as nausea and vomiting, extreme sensitivity to light, and eye pain. Cluster headaches are similar to migraine except these occur in clusters. Tension headaches are caused by muscle tension and may be relieved by massage; these headaches are not as severe as migraines. Chronic daily headaches can be caused from a number of things and specific treatment will depend on the cause of these headaches.

92. B: Hypovolemic shock is the result of a large amount of blood causing a decrease in blood pressure. While a hemorrhage is the most common cause of hypovolemic shock, the loss of interstitial fluid may also cause this type of shock. Cardiogenic shock may result from a variety of types of heart failure. Neurogenic shock results from the dilation of blood vessels, creating an unstable autonomic stimulation of smooth muscles. Anaphylactic shock is caused by an allergic reaction. A fifth type of shock includes a septic shock that is the result of septicemia, or the release of infectious toxins in the body.

93. D: Bronchitis is a lower respiratory tract infection because it occurs in the bronchi. With bronchitis, there is swelling of the bronchi due to infection and often the trachea is also infected. In these cases the disease is referred to as tracheobronchitis. This disease causes deep cough, typically with mucus and pus. Other lower respiratory tract infections include pneumonia, which is an infection in the lungs. Tuberculosis is a contagious disease that affects the lungs and surrounding tissues. Emphysema is caused from chronic bronchitis causing the alveoli to enlarge and rupture. Finally, asthma is the result of muscle spasms in the smooth muscles of the bronchial passages.

94. B: Hypernatremia is caused by sodium imbalance; specifically too much sodium. This is typically defined as above 145 mEq/L. Hypernatremia could be cause by a high salt diet and may result in dehydration or diarrhea. On the other hand, hyponatremia would be too little sodium; typically below 136 mEq/L. Sodium imbalances affect the nervous system and include symptoms such as confusion, headaches, seizures, coma, and death. Potassium imbalances include levels less than 3.8 mEq/L and above 5.1 mEq/L. Small imbalances of potassium can result in serious illnesses. Calcium imbalances include any level less than 8.4 mg/dL or more than 10.5 mg/dL. Symptoms of calcium imbalances include muscle weakness, reduced reflexes, pancreatitis, and rickets.

95. B: The purpose of the massage therapist and the massage itself is to increase cell metabolism, decrease pain, and increase range of motion. It is not to heal. All healthcare professionals must work within the scope of their practice. For a massage therapist, diagnosing and treating disease is out of their scope of practice. However, many massage techniques will help with the healing process and it is beneficial if the therapist is in communication with the client's physician if they are being treated for other illnesses or conditions. This communication will provide the client with the best possible care.

96. A: Breaking up adhesions is considered a mechanical effect of massage. Mechanical effects are the result of applying direct pressure to the body. Other ways to create mechanical effects include assisted stretching techniques. Physiological effects are those that result in physical and chemical changes in the body. For example, a massage may help flush toxins and other waste products, which would increase blood flow and cellular metabolism. Psychological effects create an emotional change in the body. With massage, stimulation of the nervous system can reduce stress and increase relaxation and well being.

97. B: The lymphatic system relies on voluntary muscle movement in order to be moved throughout the body. This movement is important, as it is the lymph that is responsible for carrying waste and toxins from cell breakdown and metabolism out of the body. Massage is beneficial with this process, as it can assist with this movement. Just as massage increases blood circulation, it also increases lymphatic circulation. In addition, the flow of lymph out of the blood stream also increases because massage tends to open closed blood capillaries through the release of histamines and acetylcholine.

98. C: A muscle spasm or cramps can occur with overstimulation of the nervous system. In order to release a muscle spasm or cramp, it is suggested that the therapist perform compressions on the tendon of the muscle. This technique activates proprioceptors, which in turn release the spasm or cramp. Other techniques include slow stretching, stimulation of the Golgi tendons, and reciprocal inhibition treatments. Golgi tendons monitor the length of the muscles and react accordingly in order to bring a muscle back to normal. If the Golgi tendon senses that the muscle is overextended, it will contract; on the other hand, if the Golgi tendon senses that the muscle is too contracted, it will relax. In addition, Golgi tendons have inhibitory effects on muscles in order to maintain the normal position of the muscle.

99. C: Effleurage or gliding is typically the first stroke of a massage. This stroke helps to warm the muscles and help relax the client. With this massage stroke, the therapist's hands are firm but relaxed, and glide easily over the muscles. This stroke can also be used with the therapist's forearms, thumbs, or fists. Therapists should keep in mind that the effleurage stroke should be consistent in speed and pressure. Other uses for this massage stroke include to apply oil, assess your client's muscles, establish your client's pressure tolerance, stimulate muscles, stretch muscles, and to increase lymphatic flow.

100. A: Petrissage or kneading focuses on the deeper tissue and may involve lifting, rolling, and compressing the deep muscles. This stroke type is used sparingly as it can be exhausting for the therapist, however, proper body mechanics can assist in endurance. Petrissage strokes also include skin rolling, fulling, and ischemic compression. Petrissage is beneficial to the client in a number of ways including, increasing the removal of metabolic waste and other toxins, release adhesions in muscle bellies, increasing the flow of fluid in deep tissue, and stretching muscle tissue and fascia.

101. A: Range of motion is the natural movement that a joint can go through. Depending on the joint, its range of motion will vary. For example, The cervical joint has a range of motion from 0-80 degrees, shoulder from 0-180 degrees, elbow 0-140 degrees, radioulnar from 0-80 degrees, wrist from 0- 60, thoracic from 0-50 degrees, lumbar from 0-60 degrees, hip from 0-100 degrees, knee from 0-150 degrees, ankle from 0-40 degrees, subtalar from 0-30 degrees, and the metatarsophalangeal from 0-50 degrees. Note that the normal range of motion will also vary for each joint depending on the type of movement (e.g., flexion, extension, etc.). When a joint has abnormal restrictions its range of motion is reduced.

102. A: Massage is indicated for the treatment of asthma, as massage may be helpful in reducing stress and loosening intercostals, thus increasing breathing. Other conditions are contraindicated for massage and could result in further injury or problems. Edema, which is swelling, can be caused by a number of things; the massage therapist should ask questions in order to figure the cause, In the cases of edema due to heart decompensations, infection, kidney ailments, or obstructions, massage is contraindicated. Bursitis is inflammation of the bursae, and massage could increase the inflammatory response. Abdominal aneurysm is contraindicated on the abdomen. The therapist can massage other parts of the body not affected.

103. B: A systemic effect of hydrotherapy will affect the entire body. For example, vasodilation causes a drop in blood pressure throughout the entire body. A therapist may create a systemic effect by applying heat for 20-30 minutes. This heat application will continue to produce effects for up to an hour after the treatment. Local effects are restricted to specific areas of the body. Reflex affects the skin and other body parts through the nervous system. The various types of effects apply to both hot and cold applications. The results will depend on the type of treatment.

104. C: The study of movement is called Kinesiology. This field is often combined with biomechanics which looks at movement in terms of mechanics. Within this field, muscles are classified or termed according to their function. Prime movers are the muscles that initiate and maintain movement. Synergists assist the prime movers. Antagonists oppose the prime movers. The combination of a prime mover and an antagonist is referred to as a fixator. There are also neutralizers that inhibit unwarranted movement while the prime mover is in action. In addition to their functional classifications, there are different characteristics of muscles, including fast, slow, and intermediate twitch muscle fibers.

105. D: Specialized testing may include passive or active range of motion (ROM), strength testing, or orthopedic testing. The purpose of specialized tests is to determine the functionality of various areas of the body. Other parts of this type of assessment include taking a history including the client's family medical history, and personal medical history. Observations are also useful and should include mood, gait, and standing and sitting postures. A final component of this assessment includes palpation, which begins with the superficial tissue and gradually moves to the deeper tissues. With palpation, the therapist will feel for symmetry, temperature, muscle tone, and texture.

106. C: Microvilli are found only in the small intestine and are organelles within the cytoplasmic membrane. The function of the microvilli is to increase the surface area of the small intestines and assist in absorption. These microvilli are a part of an extensive network of organelles that absorb fats from chime. Included in this process are lacteal, which are lymphatic vessels; plicae, circular folds; and villi, finger-like projections; all serving to increase the surface area of the small intestine and facilitate absorption. As materials enter into the small intestine, they travel through the duodenum, where most of the absorption occurs to the jejunum, and finally the ileum.

107. C: The permease system also called a cell or ion pump moves molecules against the concentration gradient. Because this movement is against the gradient, energy or ATP is required, thus it is an active transport system. Other active transport systems include pinocytosis, in which a cell will engulf liquid droplets and process them; and phagocytosis, or cell eating, in which a cell will engulf a solid molecule and process it. With phagocytosis, a cell will typically engulf bacteria or other cellular waste. Since ATP is required for these processes, the cells exert work and require chemical processes in order to create the energy required.

108. B: Amy will have to pay out-of-pocket expenses for the flood damage because she did not purchase Business & Personal Property Loss insurance. This type of insurance covers a business owner for a number of events including fires, water damage, or theft. Had Amy purchased this type of insurance, the insurance would have covered the loss of any business or personal equipment. While some events seem unlikely, it is important to understand the risks involved in owning a business as well as the precautions one can take to protect all business and personal assets.

109. B: Amy is covered in this case because she has Property Damage and Bodily Injury Liability. With this type of insurance, incidents that occur at her office including falls or slips as well as injury due to equipment failure are covered. This type of insurance is required in many states and may be specifically be required by a landlord if a therapist rents office space for their practice. In addition to covering a client in the case of an accident, this insurance protects the therapist from unwarranted bills or legal actions.

110. C: Amy did not develop a business plan. This is an essential document for any business, as it includes important information about the business, and its mission and goals. A typical business plan will include the following information: cover page, table of contents, owner's statement, executive summary, purpose and goals, a detailed description of the business, a marketing plan, risk assessment and financial analysis, operations and organizational policies, strategies for success, and other supporting information that the owner feels is necessary. While others may not read this document, it is important to have and keep updated in order to ensure you are on track with your business goals and you are able to refine these goals as the business grows.

111. B: By creating a logo and marketing materials, Amy is developing her professional image. Your professional image is the outward image presented to the public and your clients. It is important for therapists to represent themselves in a professional manner. Other ways a massage therapist can develop their professional image include keeping a clean massage room and waiting room, proper dress attire, and efficient and professional communication skills. A therapist's professional image will also expand to the therapeutic session itself, those who keep accurate notes, listen and are empathic toward their clients and respect their clients privacy show a positive professional image.

112. C: The occupational therapist would be the best referral in this case. The role of an occupational therapist is to work with clients to increase independence, thus increasing their quality of life. This type of therapist focuses on activities typically performed at work, in the home, or related to self care. It is an Occupational Therapist's job to enhance the development of their clients functioning. While you may continue to work with the client, the referral and continued communication with the other therapist would be essential in providing the client the best care possible.

113. A: Airway, Breathing, Circulation are the ABCs of First Aid. This is considered the primary survey and should be conducted immediately after finding a victim. If the individual is in any immediate danger, First Aid protocol states that you address any problem and then move on a secondary survey or assessment. The secondary survey will be more thorough and will include a full body survey to search for any injuries. It is important that both the primary and the secondary surveys are completed and are efficient as these precautions could be life-saving as the victim waits for emergency medical help.

114. B: An asymmetric standing position is the most efficient position for a massage therapist. For this position, the therapist will stand with one foot in front of the other. This will allow the therapist to leverage their own body weight into the massage. Additionally, as body weight is shifted from one foot to the other, the therapist can conserve energy. This position also protects the ankle and foot and allows for the knees to be bent throughout the massage. It is also beneficial to sit when possible while performing massage in order to conserve energy.

115. B: Passive joint movements also referred to as arthrokinematic movement occur as a result of another movement. This type of passive movement could also be considered the "play" a joint has or its ability to move freely within the joint capsule. Typically resulting after active movements, this accessory movement may slide, roll, or spin within a joint. On the other hand, active joint movements, or osteokinematic movements are voluntary and require effort to perform. For example flexing the arm is considered an osteokinematic movement. In massage, the therapist may perform various movements through stretching.

116. C: The anatomic barrier is the point at which injury would occur to a joint. Each joint's anatomic barrier will vary and is expressed as degrees for range of motion. However, because it is at this barrier that injury will occur, other barriers exist to avoid reaching the anatomic barrier. The physiologic barrier is determined by sensory functions of the nervous system. The physiologic barrier allows for full range of motion and full functionality of the joint. In addition to this barrier, there is the pathologic barrier that hinders normal range of motion. This may be expressed as stiffness or pain in the joint.

117. B: All massage therapists should have a basic understanding of the functions and dysfunctions of the human body. However, for those therapists who are interested in working with physicians or within other medical settings, it will be even more important to understand these elements of the human body. It will be in these settings that the massage therapist will encounter a variety of illnesses and dysfunctions. As such, they must understand the indications, contraindications, and precautions that must be taken for each of their clients. These therapists may choose additional training in medical massage to ensure that they are knowledgeable to practice in this specialized field.

118. C: The effects of hydrotherapy are seen mostly within the autonomic nervous system. Depending upon the temperature of the water being used for the therapy, different aspects of this system will be stimulated. For example, to stimulate the sympathetic system, the therapist will use cold water, while they will use warm water to stimulate the parasympathetic responses. Additionally, by applying heat or cold for varying periods of time, the therapist can affect the dilatation of the circulatory system. More specifically, cold application for a short period of time will stimulate the nervous system and cause vasoconstriction.

119. C: Lymphatic drainage focuses on this system and helps move various toxins out of the body. While this is done naturally, manually manipulating the lymphatic system may cause a toxin overload and affect the client, causing them to feel fatigued. There are various modifications of lymphatic drainage including techniques developed my Emil Vodder, Eyal Lederman, and Bruno Chickly. However, regardless of the style used, this is a specialized massage technique that requires additional training. Lymph moves through the body through lymph vessels that are not controlled by the heart pump. Therefore the lymph vessels must contract in order to move the lymph through. Lymphatic drainage is one way to assist this system and drain toxins from the body.

120. B: Low blood pressure is contraindicated for lymphatic drainage because this type of body work lowers blood pressure. By performing for lymphatic drainage on a client who already has low blood pressure, dizziness and fainting may occur upon standing after the bodywork. Other contraindications include illnesses; both viral and bacterial infections. These are contraindicated because the lymphatic drainage may spread the illness to other parts of the body, thus enhancing the illness. In clients with fever, lymphatic drainage lowers body temperature. Finally, this type of body work affects the client's circulation and therefore those clients with weak hearts or other heart conditions may be contraindicated for lymphatic drainage.

121. A: Palliative care focuses on making the client as comfortable as possible. In many cases those individuals in the end stages of a terminal illness will be uncomfortable and some may be in pain. As a massage therapist in this environment, you would be responsible for being empathic and respectful toward your client in order to ensure the body work was comforting and not causing additional pain. It will also be important that the therapist be in contact with the other healthcare professionals caring for the individual as well as the family.

122. D: Systems are the most complex units of the body because they consist of all other units such as cells, tissues, and organs. Systems are comprised of organs that are arranged in such a way that they are able to work together to perform specific functions. Within the human body, there are eleven systems: integumentary; skeletal; muscular; nervous; endocrine; cardiovascular; lymphatic; respiratory; digestive; urinary; and reproductive. All systems are essential for maintaining balance and health. Because organs within a system function as a whole, when one organ is dysfunctional, the entire system will be affected.

123. C: Approximately 96% of the human body is comprised of oxygen, carbon, hydrogen, and nitrogen. These elements occur naturally and are essential for the proper functioning of our bodies. In addition to these main elements, there are nearly 20 other elements that can be found in very small quantities within the body. Elements are composed of atoms combining to form molecules. In addition to these elements, they can combine, typically through a chemical reaction, to form compounds. For example, carbon dioxide is formed in the lungs. This compound is formed by the fusion of two oxygen molecules.

124. C: Red blood cells do not have a nucleus as well as no cytoplasmic organelles. Also referred to as erythrocytes, these cells are responsible for transporting oxygen and carbon dioxide. Because these cells do not have a nucleus, they are unable to reproduce and only have a life span of approximately 80-120 days. The red pigment of these cells is caused by hemoglobin which is responsible for homoeostasis. Disorders of red blood cells often occur because the body overproduces these cells, resulting in disorders such as polycythemia. Other red blood cell disorders include anemia, which comes in a variety of forms.

125. A: Squamous epithelial tissue is flat and scale-like. This type of tissue can be found in the air sacs of the lungs. This tissue is typically seen as a very thin layer and is able to absorb oxygen and pass it into the blood stream. Other tissue types include the cuboidal, which is cube shaped, columnar, which is high and wide, and transitional, which is able to stretch and therefore may vary in shape. In addition to the types of epithelial tissues, they can also be found in varying arrangements including simple and stratified.

126. A: The integumentary system includes the body's oil glands as well as the skin, hair, nails, sense receptors, and sweat glands. This system accounts for approximately 16% of the average person's body weight and may weigh approximately 20 pounds for an average-size adult. This system is the body's first line of defense against toxins and other contaminants as well as protects the organs from physical damage. The oil glands in this system serve to provide moisture to the skin. Also included in this system are sense organs and other sensors that serve to regulate the body and maintain homeostasis.

127. B: There are a number of risk factors for disease, some of which can be controlled for and some which cannot be controlled for. Those that cannot be controlled for include genetic factors. These risk factors are passed on from generation to generation in the DNA. On the other hand, risk factors such as lifestyle, stress, and environment can be controlled for. For example, lifestyle risk factors such as smoking, excessive sun tanning, and poor diet will put an individual at a higher risk of some diseases. Stress can also increase one's risk for disease. Finally, although not all environmental conditions can be controlled for, it is possible for humans to change their environment in order to reduce risk factors.

128. B: Serous membranes are found within closes cavities. This type of membrane is made up of two thin layers of tissue, one layer being simple squamous and the other layer being connective tissue. The connective tissue, which is on the bottom, serves to support cells. These membranes are named specifically based on their location in the body. For example, the serous membranes that cover body cavities are called parietal, whereas those that cover organs are called visceral. These membranes serve to reduce friction between organs by producing and releasing a lubricant.

129. C: The mucous membranes are those that open to the outside of the body. This will include the respiratory, digestive, urinary, and reproductive tracts. The makeup of mucous membranes will depend on the location of the membrane and can range from stratified squamous membranes found in the esophagus, to simple columnar membranes found in the digestive tract. These membranes remain moist due to the thick mucus of which they are comprised. In addition, the point at which the skin and the mucus membrane meet is referred to as mucocutaneous and are typically located around openings on the body.

130. C: Myofilaments are structures or units within each skeletal muscle fiber. Within each muscle fiber, myofilaments may be thick or thin. Thick myofilaments produce the protein myosin, whereas thin myofilaments produce the protein actin. Additionally, the unit of both thick and thin myofilaments is referred to as a sarcomere. As the muscle contracts the myofilaments attach and pull on each other. As the muscle relaxes, the myofilaments release. Calcium and energy, supplied by the breakdown of ATP, are both necessary for this process to work. This is also known was the sliding filament model.

131. D: There are four main muscles of the trunk and from deep to superior are transversus abdominis, internal oblique, rectus abdominis, and external oblique. The transversus abdominis, internal oblique, and external oblique muscles function to compress the abdomen and all have an insertion point at the midline of the abdomen. The external oblique muscles have an origin at the lower thoracic cage. The internal oblique muscles have an origin at the pelvis. The transversus abdominis has an origin at the ribs, vertebrae, and the pelvis. Finally, the rectus abdominis functions to flex the trunk and has an insertion at the lower rib cage and an origin at the pubis.

132. C: The Iliopsoas is not a part of the adductor group for the lower extremities. Rather, this muscle serves to flex the thigh or the trunk and has an insertion at the femur and an origin at the ilium and vertebrae. Additionally, this muscle functions to stabilize the trunk. The adductor longus, gracilis, and pectineus are all adductor muscles. The adductor longus and the pectineus have an insertion at the femur and an origin at the pubis. The gracilis has an insertion at the tibia and an origin at the pubis

133. B: The biceps femoris is a part of the hamstring group that functions to flex the knee. This muscle has an insertion at the tibia and an origin at the ischium. Other muscles in this group include the semimembranosus with an insertion at the tibia and an origin at the ischium and the semitendinosus, with an insertion at the fibula and an origin at the ischium and femur. For a runner, these muscles are very important because they work while running. Injury to muscles in the hamstring groups often occur due to strain, or overexertion of the muscle, or pulling one of the muscles.

134. C: The epiphyseal plate is not found in the long bone of an adult. Rather, what is found is the epiphyseal line. The difference between the two is that the epiphyseal plate is made of cartridge and the epiphyseal line has become ossified bone. This ossification of bone occurs during growth and once all of the cartilage has turned into bone, growth stops. Other structures in the long bone include the epiphysis (at the end), spongy bone (found in the epiphysis), red marrow (in the spongy bone), compact bone (consisting of the diaphysis), the periosteum and endosteum (outer and inner layers), and the medullary cavity (hollow inner part of the long bone).

135. B: A tuberosity is a bony landmark characterized by its large round projection. Massage therapists may use these bony landmarks to find muscles as the massage. Other bony landmarks include tubercles, which are small and knob-like, and the trochanter, which is found on the femur. Other landmarks such as a crest (ridge or bone, found on the ilium), line (less prominent than a crest, on the femur), epicondyle (raised area), spine (sharp projections), malleolus (projections which are both medial and lateral such as the ankle bones), and a process (prominent projections on a bone) can also be used to locate muscles and their attachments.

136. C: A neutralizer refers to the counteraction of one muscle in order to avoid undesired movements. On the other hand, there are five main functions of bones: first, to support the body, including the organs and the muscles; to protect the organs from injury, specifically the skull completely covers the brain and the rib cage covers the lungs and heart; to function for movement; to serve as storage for calcium; and finally, to conduct the process of hemopoiesis, the process of developing blood cells.

137. B: Pronation is the movement that will result in the palms facing toward the back when beginning in the anatomical position. In this case, by turning the arms again so the palms face forward is supination. These positions are also referred to during a massage. For example, when a client is lying face-down, they are in the prone position. When the client is laying face up on their backs, they are in the supine position. While a therapist may not use these terms when communicating with their clients, these may be referred to in the assessment and session notes as well as in consultation with other healthcare professionals.

138. B: Muscle fibers respond as all-or-none. In other words, if the muscle fiber contracts, then the entire fiber contracts fully before it can relax. A threshold stimulus refers to the minimum stimulus that can be applied to a muscle fiber before it reacts. Once the threshold stimulus is to a level where the muscle will react, it will be an all-or-none response. When discussing muscle movement, the prime mover refers to the main muscle contracting in order to move the body. At the same time the antagonist relaxes while the prime mover is contracting, facilitating the movement.

139. D: The spinal cord is a part of the nervous systems, however, not the brain. The cerebrum is located in the upper-most portion of the brain and is the largest section. This section is divided into the left and right lobes or hemispheres. The cerebellum is located posterior to the cerebrum, also has two hemispheres, and is made up of gray matter on the outside and white matter on the inside.

The diencephalon is positioned between the cerebrum and the midbrain and surrounds the third ventricle. Included in the diencephalon are the thalamus and the hypothalamus.

140. C: There are twelve pairs of cranial nerves in the human body. Eleven of these nerves originate under the brain's surface and travel down through the brain stem and spinal cord. However, the one exception is one pair of cranial nerves that begins in the cerebrum. As the cranial nerves travel through the spinal cord, they branch off from one of thirty-one segments in the spinal cord to various parts of the head, neck, and body. Moving from top to bottom, sections of the spinal cord branch off, allowing the nerves to reach the body, including the conus medullaris, filum terminale, and the cauda equine.

141. B: Deep sensory receptors are located in the muscles, tendons, and joints. The superficial receptors are located on the skin and the mucosa, and sense events such as temperature, pressures, and pain at the surface of the body. Visceral receptors, located in the viscera, sense things like hunger and visceral pain. Pain receptors will sense visceral, somatic, and referred pain. A fifth type of sensory receptor is the special receptor located in the eyes, ears, mouth, and nose, which function as our senses.

142. A: Antidiuretic hormone targets the kidney tissues. The purpose of this hormone is to reduce the excretion of water. What is occurring when this hormone is released is the kidneys are putting urine back into the blood stream. This action may be necessary if the body must conserve water, for example, in cases of dehydration. Essentially, the antidiuretic hormone comes from the posterior pituitary gland and works on the diuretic, which produces water and urine, and thus stops production. This hormone is also referred to as the "water-retaining hormone" or the "urine-decreasing hormone."

143. B: Epinephrine is produced in the adrenal medulla. This hormone targets the sympathetic nervous system. The result of this hormone being released is an increase in heart rate, blood pressure, and blood glucose levels. Additionally, breathing rate will increase as the airways dilate. Finally, individuals experience a reduction of digestion. Another hormone produced by the adrenal medulla is norepinephrine. This hormone has the same functions and actions as epinephrine. These hormones may be necessary if an individual has not eaten and their blood glucose levels drop, with the release of epinephrine, the blood glucose level will increase for a short period of time until the individual has a chance to eat.

144. C: Plasma is the liquid portion of blood. Plasma is necessary for the transport of oxygen from the respiratory organs and other vital minerals and nutrients from the digestive organs. Plasma also serves to carry waste products out of the body. Plasma makes up a large portion of the blood, approximately 55%. Within the plasma, approximately 7% is protein, 91% of the plasma is water, and the remaining 2% consists of other solutes. The remainder of the blood is made up of various cell formations called formed elements. These formed elements include platelets, leukocytes, and erythrocytes.

145. A: Providing your clients with an intake form is the best way for you to gather all necessary information. Intake forms commonly include the client's name and contact information and a brief medical questionnaire containing the most common conditions. Additionally, this form may also include the confidentiality notice which is to be signed by the client. In addition to the intake form, a therapist may choose to also ask questions if clarification on any item is necessary. It is important to take the time before a massage to learn about each client. With repeat clients, while an intake form may not be necessary every time, it will be necessary of the therapist to ask questions about any changes in their health or existing conditions.

146. A: A stone massage will result in the conduction of heat. Conduction occurs when there is direct contact and heat is transferred. Using a sauna would be an example of convection, by which heat is transferred by increasing the surrounding air temperature. As the sauna temperature increases, your body temperature will also increase. Using an ultrasound is an example of conversion. In the case of the ultrasound, energy is being converted into a different type of energy in order to create heat. These three types of heat transfer: conduction, convection, and conversion, are all examples of thermal effects of heat.

147. B: A sitz bath is a bath in which only the pelvic region is exposed to the water. There are three main types of sitz baths including a hot sitz, cold sitz, and a contrast sitz. In the hot sitz bath the client would be exposed to water temperature of 105-115 degrees Fahrenheit. Therapists must remember that the client must be comfortable with the water temperature. In a clod sitz bath, the client will be exposed to water temperatures of 55-75 degrees Fahrenheit. A contrast sitz bath will include a hot phase and a cold phase. The alteration of the hot and cold would be three minutes of hot water and 30 seconds of cold water.

148. C: Active listening is a very important communication skill. This type of listening will allow you to remember more of what the client says and will let the client know that you are listening and you care about their situation. Demonstrating caring and understanding will be an important step to developing trust in the therapist-client relationship. When this trust is developed the client will ultimately feel more comfortable with the therapist and will be able to relax more during the massage and receive more benefit from the work. While being aware of your clients' various conditions is important, tools such as the client intake form will help provide you, the therapist, with that information.

How to Overcome Test Anxiety

Just the thought of taking a test is enough to make most people a little nervous. A test is an important event that can have a long-term impact on your future, so it's important to take it seriously and it's natural to feel anxious about performing well. But just because anxiety is normal, that doesn't mean that it's helpful in test taking, or that you should simply accept it as part of your life. Anxiety can have a variety of effects. These effects can be mild, like making you feel slightly nervous, or severe, like blocking your ability to focus or remember even a simple detail.

If you experience test anxiety—whether severe or mild—it's important to know how to beat it. To discover this, first you need to understand what causes test anxiety.

Causes of Test Anxiety

While we often think of anxiety as an uncontrollable emotional state, it can actually be caused by simple, practical things. One of the most common causes of test anxiety is that a person does not feel adequately prepared for their test. This feeling can be the result of many different issues such as poor study habits or lack of organization, but the most common culprit is time management. Starting to study too late, failing to organize your study time to cover all of the material, or being distracted while you study will mean that you're not well prepared for the test. This may lead to cramming the night before, which will cause you to be physically and mentally exhausted for the test. Poor time management also contributes to feelings of stress, fear, and hopelessness as you realize you are not well prepared but don't know what to do about it.

Other times, test anxiety is not related to your preparation for the test but comes from unresolved fear. This may be a past failure on a test, or poor performance on tests in general. It may come from comparing yourself to others who seem to be performing better or from the stress of living up to expectations. Anxiety may be driven by fears of the future—how failure on this test would affect your educational and career goals. These fears are often completely irrational, but they can still negatively impact your test performance.

Elements of Test Anxiety

As mentioned earlier, test anxiety is considered to be an emotional state, but it has physical and mental components as well. Sometimes you may not even realize that you are suffering from test anxiety until you notice the physical symptoms. These can include trembling hands, rapid heartbeat, sweating, nausea, and tense muscles. Extreme anxiety may lead to fainting or vomiting. Obviously, any of these symptoms can have a negative impact on testing. It is important to recognize them as soon as they begin to occur so that you can address the problem before it damages your performance.

The mental components of test anxiety include trouble focusing and inability to remember learned information. During a test, your mind is on high alert, which can help you recall information and stay focused for an extended period of time. However, anxiety interferes with your mind's natural processes, causing you to blank out, even on the questions you know well. The strain of testing during anxiety makes it difficult to stay focused, especially on a test that may take several hours. Extreme anxiety can take a huge mental toll, making it difficult not only to recall test information but even to understand the test questions or pull your thoughts together.

Effects of Test Anxiety

Test anxiety is like a disease—if left untreated, it will get progressively worse. Anxiety leads to poor performance, and this reinforces the feelings of fear and failure, which in turn lead to poor performances on subsequent tests. It can grow from a mild nervousness to a crippling condition. If allowed to progress, test anxiety can have a big impact on your schooling, and consequently on your future.

Test anxiety can spread to other parts of your life. Anxiety on tests can become anxiety in any stressful situation, and blanking on a test can turn into panicking in a job situation. But fortunately, you don't have to let anxiety rule your testing and determine your grades. There are a number of relatively simple steps you can take to move past anxiety and function normally on a test and in the rest of life.

Physical Steps for Beating Test Anxiety

While test anxiety is a serious problem, the good news is that it can be overcome. It doesn't have to control your ability to think and remember information. While it may take time, you can begin taking steps today to beat anxiety.

Just as your first hint that you may be struggling with anxiety comes from the physical symptoms, the first step to treating it is also physical. Rest is crucial for having a clear, strong mind. If you are tired, it is much easier to give in to anxiety. But if you establish good sleep habits, your body and mind will be ready to perform optimally, without the strain of exhaustion. Additionally, sleeping well helps you to retain information better, so you're more likely to recall the answers when you see the test questions.

Getting good sleep means more than going to bed on time. It's important to allow your brain time to relax. Take study breaks from time to time so it doesn't get overworked, and don't study right before bed. Take time to rest your mind before trying to rest your body, or you may find it difficult to fall asleep.

Along with sleep, other aspects of physical health are important in preparing for a test. Good nutrition is vital for good brain function. Sugary foods and drinks may give a burst of energy but this burst is followed by a crash, both physically and emotionally. Instead, fuel your body with protein and vitamin-rich foods.

Also, drink plenty of water. Dehydration can lead to headaches and exhaustion, especially if your brain is already under stress from the rigors of the test. Particularly if your test is a long one, drink water during the breaks. And if possible, take an energy-boosting snack to eat between sections.

Along with sleep and diet, a third important part of physical health is exercise. Maintaining a steady workout schedule is helpful, but even taking 5-minute study breaks to walk can help get your blood pumping faster and clear your head. Exercise also releases endorphins, which contribute to a positive feeling and can help combat test anxiety.

When you nurture your physical health, you are also contributing to your mental health. If your body is healthy, your mind is much more likely to be healthy as well. So take time to rest, nourish your body with healthy food and water, and get moving as much as possible. Taking these physical steps will make you stronger and more able to take the mental steps necessary to overcome test anxiety.

Mental Steps for Beating Test Anxiety

Working on the mental side of test anxiety can be more challenging, but as with the physical side, there are clear steps you can take to overcome it. As mentioned earlier, test anxiety often stems from lack of preparation, so the obvious solution is to prepare for the test. Effective studying may be the most important weapon you have for beating test anxiety, but you can and should employ several other mental tools to combat fear.

First, boost your confidence by reminding yourself of past success—tests or projects that you aced. If you're putting as much effort into preparing for this test as you did for those, there's no reason you should expect to fail here. Work hard to prepare; then trust your preparation.

Second, surround yourself with encouraging people. It can be helpful to find a study group, but be sure that the people you're around will encourage a positive attitude. If you spend time with others who are anxious or cynical, this will only contribute to your own anxiety. Look for others who are motivated to study hard from a desire to succeed, not from a fear of failure.

Third, reward yourself. A test is physically and mentally tiring, even without anxiety, and it can be helpful to have something to look forward to. Plan an activity following the test, regardless of the outcome, such as going to a movie or getting ice cream.

When you are taking the test, if you find yourself beginning to feel anxious, remind yourself that you know the material. Visualize successfully completing the test. Then take a few deep, relaxing breaths and return to it. Work through the questions carefully but with confidence, knowing that you are capable of succeeding.

Developing a healthy mental approach to test taking will also aid in other areas of life. Test anxiety affects more than just the actual test—it can be damaging to your mental health and even contribute to depression. It's important to beat test anxiety before it becomes a problem for more than testing.

Study Strategy

Being prepared for the test is necessary to combat anxiety, but what does being prepared look like? You may study for hours on end and still not feel prepared. What you need is a strategy for test prep. The next few pages outline our recommended steps to help you plan out and conquer the challenge of preparation.

Step 1: Scope Out the Test

Learn everything you can about the format (multiple choice, essay, etc.) and what will be on the test. Gather any study materials, course outlines, or sample exams that may be available. Not only will this help you to prepare, but knowing what to expect can help to alleviate test anxiety.

Step 2: Map Out the Material

Look through the textbook or study guide and make note of how many chapters or sections it has. Then divide these over the time you have. For example, if a book has 15 chapters and you have five days to study, you need to cover three chapters each day. Even better, if you have the time, leave an extra day at the end for overall review after you have gone through the material in depth.

If time is limited, you may need to prioritize the material. Look through it and make note of which sections you think you already have a good grasp on, and which need review. While you are studying, skim quickly through the familiar sections and take more time on the challenging parts.

Write out your plan so you don't get lost as you go. Having a written plan also helps you feel more in control of the study, so anxiety is less likely to arise from feeling overwhelmed at the amount to cover.

Step 3: Gather Your Tools

Decide what study method works best for you. Do you prefer to highlight in the book as you study and then go back over the highlighted portions? Or do you type out notes of the important information? Or is it helpful to make flashcards that you can carry with you? Assemble the pens, index cards, highlighters, post-it notes, and any other materials you may need so you won't be distracted by getting up to find things while you study.

If you're having a hard time retaining the information or organizing your notes, experiment with different methods. For example, try color-coding by subject with colored pens, highlighters, or post-it notes. If you learn better by hearing, try recording yourself reading your notes so you can listen while in the car, working out, or simply sitting at your desk. Ask a friend to quiz you from your flashcards, or try teaching someone the material to solidify it in your mind.

Step 4: Create Your Environment

It's important to avoid distractions while you study. This includes both the obvious distractions like visitors and the subtle distractions like an uncomfortable chair (or a too-comfortable couch that makes you want to fall asleep). Set up the best study environment possible: good lighting and a comfortable work area. If background music helps you focus, you may want to turn it on, but otherwise keep the room quiet. If you are using a computer to take notes, be sure you don't have any other windows open, especially applications like social media, games, or anything else that could distract you. Silence your phone and turn off notifications. Be sure to keep water close by so you stay hydrated while you study (but avoid unhealthy drinks and snacks).

Also, take into account the best time of day to study. Are you freshest first thing in the morning? Try to set aside some time then to work through the material. Is your mind clearer in the afternoon or evening? Schedule your study session then. Another method is to study at the same time of day that you will take the test, so that your brain gets used to working on the material at that time and will be ready to focus at test time.

Step 5: Study!

Once you have done all the study preparation, it's time to settle into the actual studying. Sit down, take a few moments to settle your mind so you can focus, and begin to follow your study plan. Don't give in to distractions or let yourself procrastinate. This is your time to prepare so you'll be ready to fearlessly approach the test. Make the most of the time and stay focused.

Of course, you don't want to burn out. If you study too long you may find that you're not retaining the information very well. Take regular study breaks. For example, taking five minutes out of every hour to walk briskly, breathing deeply and swinging your arms, can help your mind stay fresh.

As you get to the end of each chapter or section, it's a good idea to do a quick review. Remind yourself of what you learned and work on any difficult parts. When you feel that you've mastered the material, move on to the next part. At the end of your study session, briefly skim through your notes again.

But while review is helpful, cramming last minute is NOT. If at all possible, work ahead so that you won't need to fit all your study into the last day. Cramming overloads your brain with more information than it can process and retain, and your tired mind may struggle to recall even previously learned information when it is overwhelmed with last-minute study. Also, the urgent nature of cramming and the stress placed on your brain contribute to anxiety. You'll be more likely to go to the test feeling unprepared and having trouble thinking clearly.

So don't cram, and don't stay up late before the test, even just to review your notes at a leisurely pace. Your brain needs rest more than it needs to go over the information again. In fact, plan to finish your studies by noon or early afternoon the day before the test. Give your brain the rest of the day to relax or focus on other things, and get a good night's sleep. Then you will be fresh for the test and better able to recall what you've studied.

Step 6: Take a Practice Test

Many courses offer sample tests, either online or in the study materials. This is an excellent resource to check whether you have mastered the material, as well as to prepare for the test format and environment.

Check the test format ahead of time: the number of questions, the type (multiple choice, free response, etc.), and the time limit. Then create a plan for working through them. For example, if you have 30 minutes to take a 60-question test, your limit is 30 seconds per question. Spend less time on the questions you know well so that you can take more time on the difficult ones.

If you have time to take several practice tests, take the first one open book, with no time limit. Work through the questions at your own pace and make sure you fully understand them. Gradually work up to taking a test under test conditions: sit at a desk with all study materials put away and set a timer. Pace yourself to make sure you finish the test with time to spare and go back to check your answers if you have time.

After each test, check your answers. On the questions you missed, be sure you understand why you missed them. Did you misread the question (tests can use tricky wording)? Did you forget the information? Or was it something you hadn't learned? Go back and study any shaky areas that the practice tests reveal.

Taking these tests not only helps with your grade, but also aids in combating test anxiety. If you're already used to the test conditions, you're less likely to worry about it, and working through tests until you're scoring well gives you a confidence boost. Go through the practice tests until you feel comfortable, and then you can go into the test knowing that you're ready for it.

Test Tips

On test day, you should be confident, knowing that you've prepared well and are ready to answer the questions. But aside from preparation, there are several test day strategies you can employ to maximize your performance.

First, as stated before, get a good night's sleep the night before the test (and for several nights before that, if possible). Go into the test with a fresh, alert mind rather than staying up late to study.

Try not to change too much about your normal routine on the day of the test. It's important to eat a nutritious breakfast, but if you normally don't eat breakfast at all, consider eating just a protein bar. If you're a coffee drinker, go ahead and have your normal coffee. Just make sure you time it so that the caffeine doesn't wear off right in the middle of your test. Avoid sugary beverages, and drink enough water to stay hydrated but not so much that you need a restroom break 10 minutes into the test. If your test isn't first thing in the morning, consider going for a walk or doing a light workout before the test to get your blood flowing.

Allow yourself enough time to get ready, and leave for the test with plenty of time to spare so you won't have the anxiety of scrambling to arrive in time. Another reason to be early is to select a good seat. It's helpful to sit away from doors and windows, which can be distracting. Find a good seat, get out your supplies, and settle your mind before the test begins.

When the test begins, start by going over the instructions carefully, even if you already know what to expect. Make sure you avoid any careless mistakes by following the directions.

Then begin working through the questions, pacing yourself as you've practiced. If you're not sure on an answer, don't spend too much time on it, and don't let it shake your confidence. Either skip it and come back later, or eliminate as many wrong answers as possible and guess among the remaining ones. Don't dwell on these questions as you continue—put them out of your mind and focus on what lies ahead.

Be sure to read all of the answer choices, even if you're sure the first one is the right answer. Sometimes you'll find a better one if you keep reading. But don't second-guess yourself if you do immediately know the answer. Your gut instinct is usually right. Don't let test anxiety rob you of the information you know.

If you have time at the end of the test (and if the test format allows), go back and review your answers. Be cautious about changing any, since your first instinct tends to be correct, but make sure you didn't misread any of the questions or accidentally mark the wrong answer choice. Look over any you skipped and make an educated guess.

At the end, leave the test feeling confident. You've done your best, so don't waste time worrying about your performance or wishing you could change anything. Instead, celebrate the successful completion of this test. And finally, use this test to learn how to deal with anxiety even better next time.

Review Video: Test Anxiety
Visit mometrix.com/academy and enter code: 100340

Important Qualification

Not all anxiety is created equal. If your test anxiety is causing major issues in your life beyond the classroom or testing center, or if you are experiencing troubling physical symptoms related to your anxiety, it may be a sign of a serious physiological or psychological condition. If this sounds like your situation, we strongly encourage you to seek professional help.

Online Resources

Due to our efforts to try to keep this book to a manageable length, we've created a link that will give you access to all of your online resources:

mometrix.com/resources719/texmassthwrex

It's Your Moment, Let's Celebrate It!

Share your story @mometrixtestpreparation